The Ethics of Labeling
in Mental Health

The Ethics of Labeling in Mental Health

KRISTIE MADSEN *and*
PETER LEECH

McFarland & Company, Inc., Publishers
Jefferson, North Carolina, and London

Acknowledgments

The authors would like to express their appreciation
to the following contributors: Roy Madsen, Barbara Madsen,
Pernille Gildsig, Jan Dananell Nielsen, Sally Madsen,
Stig Wessung, Mark Madsen, David Leech, Lizzie Davies
and Lynne Calder, *Computer One-on-One.*

LIBRARY OF CONGRESS CATALOGUING-IN-PUBLICATION DATA

Madsen, Kristie, 1958–
The ethics of labeling in mental health / Kristie Madsen
and Peter Leech.
p.   cm.
Includes bibliographical references and index.

ISBN-13: 978-0-7864-2872-4
(softcover : 50# alkaline paper) ∞

1. Mental illness—Diagnosis—Moral and ethical aspects.
2. Diagnostic and statistical manual of mental disorders.
3. Mental health services—Moral and ethical aspects.
I. Leech, Peter, 1933–   II. Title.
RC469.M346   2007
362.2—dc22   2006038282

British Library cataloguing data are available

Cover photograph ©2006 PhotoSpin.

Manufactured in the United States of America

*McFarland & Company, Inc., Publishers
Box 611, Jefferson, North Carolina 28640
www.mcfarlandpub.com*

This book is dedicated to the individuals represented here from whose life struggles we can all learn, as well as those persons who continue to experience the devastating effects of stigmatizing labels.

Table of Contents

Preface

The system of mental health services in this country is an industry that profits from the harm of labeling people as mentally disordered. What does this mean?

It can best be answered by describing what would happen to you if you were to put yourself in the position of any client who comes for psychotherapy. You would be asked by the psychotherapist to describe what is going on in your life and what has moved you to seek a psychotherapist at this time.

If you agree to work together, your psychotherapist will inform you that everything you tell him will be confidential, with the exception of any information you share that would indicate you might harm yourself or someone else. In that case, the psychotherapist is required by law to share the information with law enforcement.

You will come away with an overall impression that what you say is confidential. You may not be aware that confidential information may legally be transmitted through a variety of hands outside this office in order for you to receive services.

For example, if your fees are to be paid by any health insurance entity, within a few visits the psychotherapist is required to provide that entity with a diagnostic label. This label is supposed to define the kind of mental problem you have, and is obtained from a book that psychotherapists use entitled *Diagnostic and Statistical Manual for Mental Disorders* (DSMMD).[1]

Where is the harm? The DSMMD label will be for you like a brand burnt into the hide of an animal. It will be with you forever.

All entities require this label in order to pay your therapy fees. It will be kept as a permanent record on file in your name. It will be seen by many people as it goes into the larger system, some of whom could be your friends and neighbors or co-workers. It will be talked about as a mental disorder and interpreted as mental illness. You will never recover. The record will always be there to define you as mentally disordered.

Where is the profit? The business of developing, publishing and distributing the DSMMD has become a multi-million dollar industry worldwide. "The DSM-III and the DSM-IIIR together sold more than a million copies. Sales of the DSM-IV (1994) also exceeded a million, and the DSM-IV TR has sold 420,000 copies since its publication in 2000."[2] The publisher, apparently supported by policy makers in government and the private health insurance industry, has a monopoly on the provision of the manual.

Because the DSMMD diagnosis is required of psychotherapists who want to be paid by third party payers, all psychotherapists must have the manual available to them in order to select the most appropriate label for the hapless patient. Perusing the Internet, one can see the distribution of DSMMD books, and other DSMMD related materials, that appear in every aspect of the medical, psychotherapy and counseling professions in America and can be tracked in its distribution to many nations around the globe, some as far away as Africa. Annual sales of the DSMMD (for example, a paperback copy of the DSM-IV TR was quoted at $64 by Amazon.com, January 2005) and companion manuals to assist the user can be projected to continue in the millions of dollars each year because of the enormous dependency on it to deliver mental health services to consumers.[3]

To get a sense of how large the industry is, we contacted a representative from the American Psychiatric Association to discuss the annual sales of the DSMMD. According to our source, the sales from the years 1994 to 2000 could be calculated to be approximately forty-nine million dollars. This is a conservative estimate in that it did not include sales from outside the U.S., nor did it include sales from the list of more than forty-one publications distributed worldwide by the same publisher (of which the DSMMD is just one.) According to the representative, newer versions of the DSMMD can be expected as more scientific research emerges making it a necessity to develop a new manual.[4]

The point is, however, each year a new crop of professionals working in the field of mental health will need the manual for their jobs, licenses or degrees. It can be assumed that everyone who practices psychotherapy or who utilizes the manual in some way will be in line to purchase the newest versions. The representative was quick to point out that it is not just professionals in mental health that require the DSMMD. The manual is needed by just about everyone. That includes, of course, mental health professionals such as psychologists and social workers but also extends to schools, lawyers (particularly the ones dealing with mental illness or malpractice), insurance companies as well as some of the public who buy it out of interest. In effect, as the DSMMD has become more text-oriented and accessible since the earlier version, it has also become used directly as a text book. If one looks across the nation at federal and state money set aside each year for mental health services, public and private, along with social agencies that are connected in some way to the diagnostic process, the impact and vastness of the DSMMD empire is self evident.

Who is affected? Everyone who needs mental health services, or psychotherapy. It is a given that the DSMMD will be used as the ultimate guide on every client's mental disorder. The result of the emphasis on DSMMD labeling is that people are now being defined as their mental disorders, rather than being perceived as having encountered certain obstacles in their lives with which they are struggling.

Life experiences such as those in the case scenarios we will present illustrate the serious misfortunes that may befall certain individuals who have been mistreated by the mental health phenomenon in this country. In many instances their lives have been plagued by the designation of mental disorders which have been resolved or perhaps never existed.

While this is a book aimed for the eyes of psychotherapists, counselors, service providers, health professionals, educators and students who aspire to enter the helping professions, our hope is that the public will be interested and become better informed of the problems engendered by the labeling, or mislabeling, of clients.

There are many myths behind mental health that need to bear truth saying. The focus of this book will be to examine the process of psychotherapy within the broader context of the mental health field.

Because of the widespread use of the DSMMD by practicing therapists and community professionals, the ethics of using diagnostic labeling will be discussed as well as its influence on the core of the mental health profession. Because diagnostic labeling has also become an instrument of leverage by insurance companies to determine eligibility for their services, demands have been placed on many practicing psychotherapists to comply with eligibility standards which have eroded the very essence of the therapeutic process. Third party payers have become the driving force behind the business of manufactured health. As powerful and influential partners in the decision making of psychotherapists, they care only about business interests rather than the helping process.

Distinguishing disability from disorder, and the ramifications of misapplying these concepts in practice, will also be a central theme. Several chapters will be focused on how the DSMMD has defined and encompassed much larger social issues. These include the use of medications to treat conditions such as attention deficit–hyperactivity disorder, the use of the DSMMD in assessing children and adults for disabilities, and the use of the labeling process within institutional frameworks such as special education and vocational rehabilitation.

A section of the book will be devoted to how labeling has infiltrated the entire social service structure in the nation. The language of labels has become the basis of the dialogue used by social service agencies to communicate with one another. Often within the need for the mental health agencies to work together in collaboration with other social systems, the consumer experiences barriers to accessing essential services needed in order to survive. Consumers who approach the social system and are shuffled from one agency to another because they don't fit neatly into the labeling system experience additional system induced trauma. Case scenarios are provided in order to identify for the reader what system barriers exist, followed by a brief discussion and analysis of intervention approaches that may be used by psychotherapists in addressing the nature and scope of these problems.

The last section will address the ultimate challenge: changing the face of the American mental health system to reflect a more humane approach that will address the functional needs of people instead of the current DSMMD medical model focus on pathology. Some international perspectives will be presented. Specific steps have been outlined to propose new ways of providing mental health services with an emphasis on adequately serving individuals' serious and persistent mental illness.

As mental health professionals, we recognize that the range of issues presented in this text will be uncomfortable for many professionals already working in the field of psychotherapy. However, it is essential that mental health providers begin to understand how they may have inadvertently contributed to the disadvantage of people who are in need of assistance, yet who are unable to access the services they truly need in order to elevate themselves in our society.

Psychotherapists often serve clients the way they were trained, but in doing so do not fully understand the impact or complexity of helping as it relates to clients' lives on a daily basis. As you read about the life struggles of individuals in the case scenarios, perhaps you will begin to understand the myths, if not experience the same frustrations they do when they attempt to interface with the wall of social systems that we now recognize as the mental health system.

Kristie Madsen, MA, MSW
Peter Leech, MSW, LCSW

Individuals who nowadays seek private psychoanalytic or psychotherapeutic help do not, as a rule, consider themselves either "sick" or "mentally sick," but rather view their difficulties as problems in living and the help they receive as a type of counseling. In short while medical diagnoses are the names of genuine diseases, psychiatric diagnoses are stigmatizing labels.

—Thomas S. Szasz, MD, July 1, 1973

The Greeks, who were apparently strong on visual aides, originated the term stigma to refer to bodily signs designed to expose something unusual and bad about the moral status of the signifier. The signs were cut or burnt into the body and advertised that the bearer was a slave, a criminal, or a traitor—a blemished person, ritually polluted, to be avoided, especially in public places.

—Erving Goffman from *Stigma*

1

Making the Case Against
Diagnostic Labeling

A label does not have to be made by a professional or be based upon a professional judgment to be harmful. Just about everyone endures a label at one time or another. Receiving a negative label can be devastating for those who perceive that they are judged by others in a negative light because of a particular behavior or attribute.

The problem with labeling is that labels stick to people over time whether or not the reason for the label actually exists. Labels have power. When labels are projected onto others by someone considered to be an authority, they are more likely to be believed by those who receive them. Even more devastating is that other people in the victim's world begin to believe that the labels are true even when they are not.

The psychotherapist of today is trained exclusively in the art of diagnosis, essentially using labels to identify mental disorders. The problem is that diagnostic labeling is regarded as standard operating procedure in the world of psychotherapy. Few dare to question this approach, or the appropriateness of its use with every client or situation.

A professional may argue that a proper diagnosis of mental illness starts with identifying and labeling problem behaviors. Therefore labeling is ethical because it is mandatory for any meaningful intervention.

However, the use of labeling at all raises its own ethical issues: why is a label needed, and for what reason? The ethics of labeling often goes unaddressed, unrecognized by practicing mental health professionals because of the heavy emphasis on finding a mental disorder that will fit the person and hopefully, the problem at hand.

The label might find the person but does the label actually address the problem at hand? That is the question.

Is it always essential for mental health professionals to use labels? When does labeling create unnecessary consequences for a client, or even cross the line of abusiveness in some instances?

Of course each professional is not immune to human frailties, the temptations of money, prestige and fame. Nevertheless over time the expectation has grown that helping professionals will take an ethical stance when acting on a client's behalf. When the responsibility of decision making becomes the psychotherapist's, the client must assume that the professional will act in good faith, with sound judgment that is based on the need to assist a person with leading a more functional life.

Sound professional decision making is what ethics is about. Understanding the ethics of labeling means understanding the consequences of mishandling, misapplying or misusing diagnostic labels in practice. The issues that surround the use of labeling may be best illustrated by the following cases. Each labeling issue will be identified for the reader as well as the ramifications for those who have been touched by the diagnostic process.

Case 1

Jack's life began to become unraveled when he was notified by State Family Support Services that they were seeking ten thousand dollars in child support payments for a child he never knew existed, born to a mother he had not seen since he was in his late teens. Because Jack was unable to come up with the money he was labeled a delinquent father, and his driver's license was revoked.

Without the ability to drive Jack could not continue to work as an independent landscaper. His meager savings were quickly exhausted. He lost his new truck, necessary to carry his tools for work, and his apartment.

Because of his inability to find work, or to receive unemployment benefits due to being self-employed, Jack fell into a deep depression. In order to avoid homelessness, he moved into an apartment with a friend. But his anger about his situation got out of control, he struck his friend, was arrested and sent to jail. In jail, he was seen by a psychiatrist, and told he was bi-polar and started on medication.

After his release from jail, Jack was concerned about his homelessness and the fact that the drugs for his bi-polar disorder were consumed. Jack had no money to pay for additional drugs.

Jack sought help from the mental health agency in town only to be told that he could not be served by them unless he was "a danger to himself or someone else." He went away without services or any way to access the drugs he needed to keep his life on track.

Upon appealing to the DMV to get his license to drive re-instated, Jack was told that he was too big a risk on the road and needed an eye exam to clear his glasses. Because he had no money for the eye examination, he was refused a driver's license.

Jack applied to HUD housing and was told that he needed to be seeing a therapist in order to qualify for their housing services because of his mental health history.

Again Jack appealed to mental health and was told that he needed to be on Medicaid so that the clinicians could get paid. Also, mental health professionals refused to meet with him or to provide him with a new prescription for the drugs he needed and would not consider looking at his mental health report.

Jack grew increasingly despondent about his homelessness, the loss of his license to drive, his inability to work to support himself, his inability to pay the back child support, and the inability to access the services he needed. Jack dropped out of sight and committed suicide thereafter.

Labeling Issue: The American mental health system is revered as the primary organizational entity designed to address the needs of individuals with a diagnosis of serious mental illness. However, Jack's case illustrates the ineffectiveness of the mental health system to respond to a person already diagnosed with mental illness. It also shows the futility of diagnostic labeling for individuals like Jack in managing the functional challenges in practical life settings.

Case 2

No one quite knew how to help Barry find and keep a job. He was in special education throughout his formative years and was diagnosed with severe language learning disabilities. When he got older he carried these life challenges into every social setting. He was in and out of therapy trying to cope with the loss of jobs and relationships. The therapists too were at a loss as to how to assist Barry, who was lost within a variety of social systems. No one knew how to serve him in an effective way. As time went on, Barry was seen by a psychiatrist in the community, who knew nothing about Barry's past experiences as a learning disabled individual and chose not to concern himself with Barry's past history. During the interview stage, no attention was paid to Barry's language deficits.

Labeling Problem: The psychiatrist's orientation toward mental illness contributed to his diagnosis of a new disorder and a disregard of Barry's underlying disabling condition and how it might affect his outward behavior and ability to process the psychiatrist's questions.

Ramifications: Barry is now on drugs, having a more difficult time processing information, failing in his efforts to find and keep a job, struggling with life challenges and still going to therapy to "straighten out his life."

Case 3

Ray was homeless, and had been diagnosed in his twenties with bipolar disorder and dyslexia. He had worked off and on for years at various jobs and used a variety of social service programs. Ray got jobs easily but lost them because of his temper. He could not afford the cost of lithium for his bi-polar disorder, which he needed to stabilize his mood and his life. Because Ray wanted to attend college, he approached the Department of Vocational Rehabilitation for financial support. The counselor there was skeptical about Ray's abilities to complete a college degree because of his "diagnosis of mental illness" and his inability to meet the reading and writing requirements of college due to his being "dyslexic." However, the counselor agreed to fund Ray's education and medication for a trial period. Highly motivated, Ray managed well through his first year, but felt he needed a voice synthesized computer to help with the demands of reading and writing papers. His counselor did not agree with his choice of academic program and did not want to pay for computer technology because she did not believe he would finish the course of study. Ray and his counselor argued and could not agree on anything. Ray avoided making contact with the counselor. Eventually, Ray's case was dropped by the Department of Vocational Rehabilitation. With the lack of financial support, Ray could not afford to pay for his medication. He continued to go to class. One day, however, Ray's anger got the best of him. Without lithium, he was no longer stable emotionally and he became verbally threatening to a teacher. Ray was suspended from college.

Labeling Problem: Ray's counselor approached this situation with the expectation that a person diagnosed with mental illness and dyslexia could not succeed in college. In doing so she ignored that maintaining his medication and obtaining computer technology could have assisted with his functional limitations and supported his success.

Ramifications: Ray resumed his pattern as a homeless person, and he eventually disappeared.

Case 4

Naomi had Hepatitis C. She was too sick to work and was fired from her job because of many absences due to illness. She applied twice for

Supplementary Security Income (SSI) and was rejected on the basis of not having a severe diagnosis. Her serious health problems were not considered severe enough for her to qualify for benefits. Financially destitute, needing housing and money for food, Naomi was desperate. She went to a local therapist in the area whom she knew through local group therapy meetings. Naomi explained to the therapist that SSI did not consider Hepatitis C to be severe enough to qualify under their standards. The two of them decided that the therapist would write a report for SSI diagnosing Naomi's condition as a serious mental disorder. Naomi re-applied to SSI. She received notification from SSI that she had been approved on the basis of having severe mental illness.

Labeling Problem: The therapist was forced into the position of compromising her professional decision making in order to assist Naomi to get SSI by speciously labeling Naomi as having a serious mental disorder.

Ramifications: Even though Naomi now receives SSI, her life has not improved since she received the diagnosis of mental illness. As a result of being saddled with the label from the therapist, Naomi continues to receive interrogatory calls from the SSI representatives requiring her to justify her status, her home, her financial situation. Naomi is too poor to continue to pay for HUD housing, emotionally exhausted from trying to defend her position to SSI, and too sick to return to work. Ironically, she continues to receive mental health counseling on the basis of being clinically depressed.

Case 5

Gary was a sixteen year old with a hearing impairment who was attending high school but could not concentrate in class. He had trouble listening to what the teacher said, especially when her back was turned. His grades were mediocre or worse. Life at home was not good either. He argued constantly with his overly critical father. Gary grew to hate school because many of the teachers did not understand his difficulties, especially when it came to math. He started coming late to class because it irritated his teacher and in time he made friends with other school outcasts, who were all experimenting with drugs. Gary could not resist smoking marijuana and tried cocaine once or twice. Gradually, Gary's addiction to marijuana became known to his peers and teachers. He was suspended twice for smoking in the bathrooms and forced to take drug tests on a regular basis. His attention problems were recognized, but the school psychologist did not want to have him tested for attention deficit disorder because he did not want to address the question of accommodations in the last year of high school or publicly have to reveal to Gary's parents that no accommodations had been made in the classroom for his hearing impairment. When it came time for graduation, he had several classes to make up because of his absences. The teachers got together and labeled his real problem as that of a drug user to describe his non-compliant behavior and laziness, and did not indicate that there were any underlying issues.

Labeling Problem: School professionals labeled Gary as a drug user which interfered with addressing his real functional issues, his hearing impairment, attention and concentration problems, and residual learning difficulties.

Ramifications: Gary withdrew from high school, stayed in his bedroom and became more and more anxious about his life. His parents took him to a local psychiatrist who diagnosed him as having obsessive compulsive disorder.

Case 6

Katie was a senior at a four-year university about to graduate in psychology with a 4.0 grade-point average. Years earlier she had been diagnosed with dissociative disorder but had substantially recovered from this illness, which was noted in her diagnostic report. Now she only occasionally experienced concentration problems when she was under extreme pressure to perform. Katie asked her instructors for extended test times as an accommodation for her disability limitations. Her psychology professors discussed the matters behind closed doors and decided that it was important to see her psychological report before any decisions were made. Katie felt she had nothing to hide and gave them the report to review. The professors declined her request for accommodation on the basis that she once had a prior history of dissociative disorder.

Labeling Problem: Based on the label of her prior history the faculty made the assumption that she should not become a mental health professional or work in the field. Once diagnosed with a mental disorder, the assumption is that one will always have the mental disorder, that there is no such thing as recovery. In addition, the fact that Katie's previous label of mental illness was known caused, in effect, the psychology faculty to treat her in a discriminatory fashion.

Ramifications: Katie's requests for accommodation were denied and the faculty told her that if she pursued a graduate program in psychology at another university, they would contact the graduate program and tell them that she had serious mental illness and should not be allowed to continue in the field. As a result, Katie was forced to move into another academic field.

Case 7

Mark was graduating from a social work program after four years of hard work at a university. He had been diagnosed with a mathematics disability but had maintained a 3.75 grade point average. He was hoping to get a master's degree in social work the following year. Mark was accepted to a graduate program on the basis of his school record. However, when it came time to draft his letter of intent to the social work graduate faculty, he made the mistake of writing down that he had a Specific Learning Disability affecting mathematics and that he might need accommodations. Two weeks after he had received his letter of acceptance, Mark received another letter from the graduate school stating that the faculty had decided that there were too many people contending for the same position and they had given his position to another student.

Labeling Problem: Individuals who disclose their diagnosis of disability or mental illness are vulnerable to the stigmatization and discrimination by others on the basis of the label.

Ramifications: Mark was denied the opportunity of earning a master's degree at the university.

Case 8

Tara was promoted at a mental health agency where she worked and was told that she would supervise the new unlicensed trainees in the program. Tara was holding onto a secret of her past, however. Some years before, she had been diagnosed and treated for manic depression. Now she had a lot of responsibility. Her supervisor, who had never liked her, was searching for reasons for the administrative staff to demote her. Tara lived from day to day frightened that her supervisor would find out about the previous diagnosis. Tara recognized that she had indicated on her job application that she had never been treated for a mental illness, because she felt that she had fully recovered and would be turned down because of the label.

Labeling Problem: Tara was right to be concerned about being labeled with a mental disorder. Labels continue to be used to diminish the lives of individuals long after they have received treatment and recovered.

Ramifications: Much to the surprise of her co-workers and trainees, Tara abruptly resigned from her position.

Case 9

Harry was diagnosed with a Specific Learning Disability in the third grade. His teacher had asked him to read in front of class. Harry refused because he felt that the other students would make fun of him. He put up a storm of resistance and fought with his teacher, calling her an obscene name, which landed him in the principal's office. The principal decided that Harry's educational needs would be best served in the school's alternative placement room, the self-contained classroom for emotionally disturbed children. The school psychologist agreed that Harry might learn better in a smaller setting away from his peers. As time went on, however, the school staff needed to decide what to do with him. The ethical dilemma for the school psychologist was whether he should return Harry to the regular classroom against the desires of the principal and teachers, or to rediagnose Harry as having emotional disturbance so he could remain in the self-contained classroom. The principal and the teachers took the position that the self-contained classroom was the most appropriate placement because, "Harry's defiant and intrusive behavior had caused him to be removed from the regular classroom in the first place." The school psychologist did not know what to do.

Labeling Problem: The school psychologist was forced to confront an ethical dilemma, which was whether to create a false diagnosis in order to solve a social problem, or to return Harry to the regular classroom and deal with Harry's disability and related social issues.

Ramifications: Harry remained in the alternative placement and carried the stigma of being emotionally disturbed.

Case 10

Craig was born deaf and attended a private day school for the disabled. Years before, doctors had diagnosed Craig as autistic and told his parents that he was too cognitively impaired to lead an independent life. His parents sent him to a home for other autistic children. Craig grew up isolated and learned characteristic rocking behaviors from his autistic peers. When he turned sixteen, a psychiatrist evaluated him and found that he was of normal intelligence, discovered that his autistic behavior was the result of copying his autistic peers and the real source of problems was deafness. Craig continued to show brilliance at drawing buildings and animals but was emotionally withdrawn.

Labeling Problem: Craig was misdiagnosed initially as autistic. Reliance on an inaccurate label led other professionals to ignore his essential functional limitations and abilities.

Ramifications: After years in isolation, Craig was re-diagnosed as emotionally disturbed, placed in a home with other mentally challenged adults and still lacks the ability today to communicate with anyone.

Case 11

Jason was born with cerebral palsy and was tested at age five hy a noy
chologist. Th~~~ ~ ~ ~

program to meet Jason's needs. For the next four years, however,
Jason stayed in a corner of the Self-Contained Special Education classroom without social interaction or stimulation for most of the day. When
he began to cry all the time, no one could figure out why. One day, the
special education aide noticed he was crying and took him out of his wheelchair. Immediately he stopped crying. The aide was so impressed by this
that she began to work with Jason daily around his needs to get out of his
chair. She discovered that he had some limited ability to control his own
movements and showed the results of their work together to the special
education teacher and the speech therapist. The speech therapist was not
excited about the results and demanded that the principal get rid of the
aide. She explained that Jason had "no brain," and therefore it was a waste
of school money and time to keep an aide who was working on false hopes
and school time. A dispute between the speech therapist and the special
education teacher grew. As a result, another psychologist was called to the
school to re-evaluate Jason. The psychologist determined that Jason had
been born with normal intelligence.

Labeling Problem: When Jason was labeled at age five as having "no
brain to work with," other people in his world began to believe that the
label was true and treated him accordingly. Professionals can and do make
wrong diagnoses but it is the labels that lead to devastating consequences
for individuals such as Jason. Other factors that could have contributed
to the initial misdiagnosis include inadequate professional training, nar-
rowness of professional orientation and utilization of inappropriate assessment instruments.

Ramifications: Because Jason had received little stimulation over the
years, he would continue his life with limited ability to communicate with
the outside world.

Case 12

Laurel was a fifty-year-old woman who was born profoundly deaf. At
age three, her parents were told by the doctor that she was retarded and

that in his opinion, there was no point in sending her to school unless she could learn to speak. Laurel's parents believed the doctor's conclusions and kept her at home while her siblings went to school. Laurel spent most of her childhood alone, yearning to go to school. Her parents insisted that she work around the house as if she was their personal maid. Over time Laurel became very emotionally dependent on family members for their approval. Moreover, she began to believe that she was indeed retarded. She had no expectations that she would ever live on her own or be self sufficient. As Laurel grew older, her parents paid a speech therapist to teach her spoken English. This was a difficult challenge for Laurel but she achieved results and also learned to read. Although she had achieved well beyond the expectations of her family, at age forty-five, Laurel still believed that she was retarded. She resisted learning to drive because she felt inadequate, preferring instead to rely on family members. She struggled with the idea of taking a bus on her own, voting independently and would not consider that she could obtain her own apartment with SSI money and live independently away from her parents. When Laurel turned fifty, her parents died leaving Laurel traumatized. She did not know what to do with the rest of her life. Her life had always been defined for her by other people. Laurel was in crisis. Her siblings were choosing to move away from the area, leaving her to wonder how she would survive.

Labeling Problem: Although the label that Laurel was given at age three (that she was retarded) was eventually born out as untrue over time, Laurel continued to believe and live her life as if the label was true. Professionals who use labels do negatively influence the lives of other people. As with this case, victims who internalize these labels may experience life long devastating consequences.

Ramifications: Laurel moved in with one of her siblings and continues to live in fear of developing an independent life.

Case 13

Alma was a young woman in her twenties who experienced significant limitations as the result of a spinal cord injury. She had received rehabilitative services in order to live independently but also required personal care attendants and medically related services and supplies. Alma received SSI monthly and Medicaid health insurance benefits. It was not enough to make ends meet and while Alma realized that working would conflict with SSI requirements, she also realized that she was barely getting by. Alma was bright and had the desire to find something to do with her time. She eventually found a small volunteer part-time staff position in town. As time went on, Alma earned a little bit of money for her time on the job, which supplemented what she received from SSI and it was just enough to meet her monthly expenses. Because the organization needed to report Alma's earnings, SSI was soon informed that she had a job and began to question whether Alma should continue to receive SSI. The law at that time was that if a person exceeded earnings of $230 a month, the person was no longer considered disabled under the law since the definition of disability under the law was that "a person is unable to work." Of course $230 a month would never be enough to make up for the amount she received from SSI each month, plus her medical and personal care attendant expenses. Weeks went by before Alma received notice that she was declared ineligible for SSI on the basis of her work record. Alma appealed the decision and was extremely frightened about the fact that a right was being pulled out from under her. While the appeal was ongoing Alma continued to receive benefits. After a time, however, the appeal was denied and her benefits were terminated. Although Alma vigorously contested the decision, her efforts were firmly resisted and she became more and more despondent about her situation.

Labeling issue: Using labels to define criteria for disbursement of social services sadly illustrates how agencies now operate under the law. The laws themselves re-enforce the use of labeling, in which individuals must prove their worthiness to qualify for existing services. Even individuals like Alma who have obvious physical disabilities can be cast out of the system for failure to comply with the standards associated with the label. In this case, it was Alma's failure to fit the definition of the label, "Disabled" under Federal and State law. The SSI system has become so rigidly defined by the label that it can not tolerate any person under financial duress, trying to supplement their limited income in order to survive. Notice that the functional limitations of Alma's disability were ignored and did not qualify her for SSI. Her personal care attendant and medical needs were not considered relevant to her financial situation, nor taken care of in a way that she could comply with current law and survive.

Ramifications: Eventually, the fear of losing financial supports and her own despondency about her situation contributed to Alma's decision to commit suicide and she did so successfully.

Myth I

The Mental Health System Truly Serves the Public Good

Introduction: The Myth of Serving the Public Good

Mental health professionals are often entrusted with the public good, to present the image of moral leaders in our communities, and are regarded as persons who will always uphold ethical standards, and do right rather than do harm to the weak, mentally unfit, or physically disabled.

Ethics are usually generated out of the need to convey an attitude or belief about how the public good should be served. Every professional field has its own ethics. Most have some form of the "do no harm" ethic as a way of protecting those who are most vulnerable in our society from being exploited.

Because psychotherapists have that same sense of power that comes with public trust, there is a general assumption that every professional will operate in an ethical manner resulting in decisions that will better the lives of the clients served. This, however, does not always come to pass. As you will be able to ascertain in the story below, the psychologist displayed a myriad of questionable ethics.

Jerry Jones drove an eighteen-wheel truck transporting manufactured houses across the country. He had a wife and two children who relied on him and waited patiently at home for the money each month to pay rent on their mobile home.

Although Jerry and his wife had their ups and downs, overall the couple seemed quite happy together and shared a lifestyle that included attending parties on a regular basis and bar hopping. Nothing, however, prepared them for what lay ahead.

One day Jerry was driving on a thickly-iced road on a narrow mountain highway when he had an accident that put him in the hospital. When Jerry regained consciousness, he did not remember any of the details of the event, nor the fact that he lived in a different state.

After time passed and his memory began to return, he called his wife. She announced that she was about to divorce him. She had been there to visit with her children and in her words she would rather "skip the country and become a stripper than remain hostage to a situation with a paralyzed man who is never expected to walk again."

Jerry did walk again, although not immediately. He was placed in a cognitive rehabilitation clinic and assessed daily for his ability to function independently. Vocational rehabilitation was willing to evaluate him at the clinic but was skeptical as to whether he would ever recover enough from brain damage to return to work.

Jerry not only fought his way clear of wheelchairs, walkers and canes but vowed that no one was going to stop him from getting back his job, his children, his way of life. He was angry over his wife's decision to leave him. He was also angry that she had decided to file for full custody of their two children and he called her on the phone to discuss the matter.

Jerry's wife informed him that she had contacted an attorney and the two were planning what they would do next with her part of the settlement that Jerry's employer had agreed to. Much to Jerry's surprise there had been a hearing while he was still in a coma in the hospital.

The judge had decided, on the basis of a psychologist's report, that he would never recover, agreed that he was mentally incompetent to make decisions, and appointed Jerry a conservator empowered for the rest of his life to manage his portion of the money from the settlement. Jerry's ex-wife received her share of the settlement as a part of the divorce and the attorneys and the psychologist split up the remaining money. Jerry was enraged.

When Jerry asked how it had been decided that he could not sign for himself, his wife stated as a matter of fact: "Jerry, we just had your attorney sign on your behalf. There was nothing more to do, everything had been decided for you. The judge decided you were too mentally incompetent to make your own decisions because of your condition."

Jerry slammed the phone down and promptly called his attorney. How could this happen to him? Jerry's attorney explained that Jerry had been through an evaluation by the psychologist at four months post-injury to assess the cognitive damage done to his brain. The psychologist had assessed Jerry at the most vulnerable time in his life. He had concluded that Jerry would never recover the way of life he had before. It was all included in the report—the assessment and the recommendation for the judge to appoint a conservator.

Jerry was outraged by the entire settlement arrangement. The lawyers and the judge had passed him a life sentence whereby he could not manage his own affairs for the rest of his life. He was also angry that his money would be controlled by someone else.

As he looked objectively at the situation the attorney presented, he realized that his ex-wife had received a sizeable advance on the settlement, as had the lawyers. There was no reversing the damage that had been done as a result of the psychologist's report.

Jerry paid the psychologist a visit to inquire why he could have declared him forever mentally incompetent to manage his own affairs. The psychologist answered, "I thought you would never be able to function, let alone stand independently. I thought I did right by you. You don't really want to work again, do you?"

Jerry called his ex-wife to tell her he wanted to return to work, that he wanted vocational rehabilitation to pay for his re-training and that he wanted half custody of their children. Jerry's wife said, "Just try it. You won't succeed because I told them you were an alcoholic and vocational rehabilitation won't take you as long as you are drinking." Jerry argued, "I am not drinking now and don't plan to. I plan to be re-evaluated."

Jerry called his attorney. Jerry's attorney admitted that the outlook for his life was bleak; that Jerry would never return to work again as long as the mental health professional's evaluation remained the same.

Again Jerry went back to ask the psychologist to consider the fact that eight months later the results might be different. The psychologist stated, "I can't undo what has been done. The judge asked me to be certain before he appointed a conservator to your case. To go back on that now would leave you financially vulnerable and you might not be a vocational rehabilitation candidate because of your drinking, anyway."

Jerry asked, "Does everyone know that I used to drink?" "Just about everyone," the psychologist replied. "That is why your ex-wife asked that you not manage the money that would go to your children."

Jerry thought for a minute and then asked, "Are you saying that I am the same person you evaluated while I was in the hospital? The psychologist answered, "Pretty much, but I got you a good deal for the rest of your life."

Feeling stunned, Jerry left the psychologist's office. "A good deal for the rest of your life," pounded in his ears like a drum. Jerry began to drink again. This became his pattern for the next twenty years. Jerry declined in health and never was able to work again. His label became the fact.

The Ethics of Professional Decision Making

Because the events of the above story are true, it is important to ask the question as a helping professional, what has happened here? How is it that a mental health professional, someone in whom the public would normally place trust, could be involved in decision making that would add to the devastation in Jerry's world? Was the psychologist actually working in Jerry's behalf? Did any of his decisions improve or enhance Jerry's life situation?

At some feeling level each person might be internally aware that Jerry's rights were violated, ignored, or exploited for the benefit of others. In the end, however, the reader is left to ponder the harsh reality that Jerry's life became a mirror of the attitudes and beliefs with which he was surrounded. If you were to look to the psychologist's diagnostic report to answer the questions of Jerry's dilemma, it is impossible not to pay attention to your own conscience about the injustice of the situation.

Psychotherapists must be able to evaluate their own ethical positions and examine ethical dilemmas that arise as part of their practices. Jerry's situation, however, raises the types of issues that most professionals would rather not encounter. Nevertheless, it is important to examine the right questions. Who was helped or harmed by the professional decision-making in Jerry's case? How could such a report by the psychologist wield such a powerful blow of influence that it would define the rest of Jerry's life? What criteria were the bases for professional decision making?

Was the professional's decision accurate and commensurate with Jerry's functional abilities, especially a number of months after Jerry's recovery? Who would make that determination?

How could Jerry challenge the labels he was given: alcoholic and mentally incompetent to look after his personal affairs? Is there any way for Jerry to challenge the very essence of the psychologist's report?

Could Jerry ever recover enough to return to work again? Who might be able to determine this? What would it take for Jerry to recover the same rights he enjoyed in his former life? Who or what was standing between Jerry and his future goals?

It is difficult to find evidence that the psychologist adhered to "do no harm" principles. He obviously was unconcerned about the labels he was inflicting on Jerry. He apparently had no idea of the devastating consequences on Jerry of using phrases such as "mentally incompetent." One can only assume that most psychologists today would approach Jerry's situation differently, make other decisions than the ones employed by the psychologist in the story.

What can be said is that professional judgments can be wrong. Sometimes these judgments lead to assumptions about clients that are false. Diagnostic labeling only complicates the picture even more, raising questions about what consumers have the right to expect of mental health professionals.

Do psychotherapists, when given that sense of trust to serve clients responsibly, make choices that serve the public good? Or, does a mental health system that requires diagnostic labeling put psychotherapists in the position of compromising their own ethics which could lead to a client's misfortune, or termination of a client's most beloved and important civil rights?

2

What We Believe About
Helping Professionals

Because mental health therapists are viewed as their stereotypes, portrayed as they are in the media as omniscient, immune to mental illness themselves and God-like in their ability to assess mental illness in others, it is no surprise to hear the answer to the question, "Why don't you go see a therapist?" The lay person is heard saying, "I don't need a head shrink to tell me what is the matter. I can solve my own problems without the help of some quack."

Beyond the skepticism, therapists are often revered as secretive magicians or "shrinks" who "play with the mind." Therapists are given attributes such as possession of rare insights or unusual abilities that reveal to common people their deepest dark secrets or intentions. Exceptional telepathic abilities to read a person's mind are thought to enable the therapist to determine in a moment an inadequacy, even upon a first encounter with an individual.

The act of asking for help automatically puts the lay person in a dependent role or, in the client's point of view, an inferior posture. In a society that denies having feelings or interprets having problems as a sign of weakness in an individual, going to a therapist may mean admitting that one is not perfect or is a failure at solving problems in life.

Being strong, never showing any weakness, is important in a competitive, capitalistic culture. Crying is usually seen as a sign of "breaking down," or "losing control" of one's emotions.

In some of the more affluent strata of American culture it can be considered fashionable to have one's special therapist, almost seen as a status

24

symbol to one's life. The individual who is really financially powerful and secure in society's upper class can use the therapist almost as an astrologer to improve the emotional or relationship horizon line.

In most social milieus, however, seeing a therapist for help is an act of submission, and perhaps, failure to live up to one's own expectations. Being viewed as mentally ill by other people is the most lethal condemnation that a person asking for help needs to hurdle.

Given that these dynamics are already operating, the client enters into the relationship with the therapist that is un-equal from the start. Average problems in the popular culture are not considered good reasons for seeking out the help of a therapist.

In some social circles individuals create a wall of secrecy around them so they will not be judged by family or condemned by friends or employers for associating with "the voodoo workers." The client never wants to be snickered at as being a fool who is going to someone who has a black bag of quick-fix tools or magic potions, or someone similar to the traveling miracle doctors of the Old West.

Skepticism or inaccurate imaging of professionals eludes the true understanding of the therapeutic process. The client must go into the relationship with the therapist admitting on some level that he is dependent, powerless to change his world and inadequate at finding his own solutions to his problems without the aid of a professional.

What Is in a Label?

Perceptions about people usually precede the reality of who they are. Psychotherapists in particular are given too much or too little validation as legitimate working people. Other helping professionals who work in related human service fields are also not well understood and are regarded with a certain amount of suspicion depending upon what client expectations are.

The image suffers mightily by the label, in this instance the professional title. For example psychologists and psychiatrists have an image problem of being human judges of inadequacy; they are perceived as immune to their own human frailties. They have the power to label mental disorders and treat the difficult to understand and scary population, the "mentally ill." We are all a little scared that we too will be branded mentally ill by these people.

Counselors have been given a bad rap across the board as helping professionals. Perhaps it is worth noting that the term counselor appearing here in the text is not being referred to in the broadest sense of the definition that is, as one would refer to one's lawyer as a counselor. The type of counselor referred to here is an individual who is part of the mental health system and is certified or possessing credentials as a counselor.

Returning to the discussion, counselors are often confused by the general public as providing the same service to clients as psychotherapists. Yet they do not in fact provide the same service.

Counselors work in various important capacities within each community. They may possess a mixed bag of different academic degrees, a variety of credentials or licenses, which may or may not qualify them to provide psychotherapy to clients. However, the point really is that no serious psychotherapist really wants to be called a counselor because of the characterization of being more of an advice giver or coach rather than engaging in serious psychotherapy.

It is unfortunate that counselors are viewed as less scientific and, essentially, as problem solvers. Their image suffers from being perceived by other professional peers as distributors of public services, as if that type of mission was, somehow, less worthy than their own, for example, vocational counseling. Seldom are counselors regarded with the same esteem as those professionals having medically based degrees (for example, psychiatrists or neuro-psychologists.)

Licensed clinical social workers (L.C.S.W.) fare even less positive return. No one in the general public is aware of what their title means or that they possess the skills to conduct psychotherapy in the same way as psychologists.

The title psychotherapist is used more commonly by L.C.S.W.s so that people ask for the service. Psychotherapist, however, is a scary term in that people equate the first part, "psycho," with "crazy person." Subliminally, this transfers to "therapist for psychos" with which no one wants to be associated.

Because of the purity of the god-like role of doctors in our culture, people generally don't know what to make of therapists. It is not un-natural to be suspicious of a profession that "profits off the backs of peoples' problems." Everywhere in our culture there is the idea of people taking advantage of one another usually at the expense of someone. People who desire to help others and charge for their services add to the confusion over the nature of the profession, for example, helping people in need. Taking money in exchange for goodness does not seem right somehow! A profession that capitalizes on human frailty will be open to scrutiny for sure.

Perceptions of the public have evolved over time. Unfortunately these perceptions have turned into an attitude of skepticism about helping professionals in general. How pervasive the skepticism is no one can say, but even in conversations with others one can hear comments such as:

"Aren't most shrinks screwed up themselves?"

"Should I pay for a service when I hear all the talk of certain therapists screwing their clients?"

"Aren't these people really taking advantage of people in trouble?"

"Will I really get something for my money if it costs so much each time I go?"

"Will it hurt me in the long run if others at my job find out I have been to a therapist?"

Like any profession, the field is full of persons who disguise their character imperfections or mental defects with perfect ethics. Helping professionals are not immune to human frailty. The general public continues to be suspicious of the true intentions of a skilled therapist. The challenge for any therapist is to be able to rise above the skepticism, but how?

An element of truth lies in what the public believes about the helping professional and the business of helping in general. That is, the helping professional of today does operate at the expense of the client.

Nevertheless, the consumer also has to understand the underlying expectations that are inherent in the role of being today's therapist. The very nature of the role has changed, expanding to include professional requirements imposed by a much larger, more callous mental health system.

Defining the Role of Today's Psychotherapist

Over time the field of psychotherapy has certainly grown to include many styles of practice. Public perceptions convey a residual skepticism that shroud therapists in a sea of popular myths. Some of the myths that define today's therapist include: The perfect psychotherapist arrives at the perfect diagnosis because of his or her skill and expertise at identifying mental illness; The perfect therapist specializes in fitting the client to the perfect label; A perfect therapist can find any justification for the label given, to secure a treatment plan for the client; The perfect therapist is able to justify any diagnosis by emphasizing the client's negative behaviors. But can the perfect therapist differentiate an average problem the client has from the assumed pathology of the client?

The current therapeutic process includes ingredients that will lead to an upset stomach. Therapists are taught that every client must have a DSMMD label assigned, documented, and justified by the categories cited in the DSMMD manual. With use of the DSMMD, the psychotherapist assumes that the client is the sum total of the pathology. The client's way of functioning in the world is considered derivative of the pathology as well. A homeless person is thus assumed to be pathological because of the way he is deviant from the popular culture.

People are not considered to be shaped by the external world or personal experience. There is something puritanical about believing that whatever befalls the individual is the result of their own behaviors or illness. This philosophy upholds the old notion that somehow people have earned or deserve their own misfortune.

The inability to function in an oppressive world is not viewed by the therapists committed to the DSMMD as a reason for a person to be depressed or in need of therapy. There are, for example, those professionals that hold onto a stereotype about the homeless: that they would not be in their situation were it not for their mental illness. This presumes that people who are homeless have chosen to live on the streets because "homeless people are always mentally ill."

With this attitude in mind about the disadvantaged, it is a logical leap that a client served by this type of therapist will begin to believe in the diagnosis of mental illness, deserving of the label because "my therapist said so." Yet such presumptions are the result of social prejudice and not professional expertise. The professional can always justify a position about the client by fitting the DSMMD classifications to the person. The professional's bias becomes the root of the diagnosis rather than objective observation about the "person in environment" relationship. Why look any farther? People are their label, right? Looking through the lenses of pathology at such a homeless individual, the therapist can easily conclude that all the behaviors of the individual can be interpreted the same way, even if the behavior parallels the behaviors one can find in all of mankind.

In the mid-fifties Erving Goffman, a sociologist, did some of his field work at a mental institution where he noted that the institution, not the illness, was the most significant factor in creating a mental hospital patient.[1] He observed that the patient's reactions are similar to those of inmates who are defined by other institutions such as prisons or the military. A prisoner, for example, begins to be shaped by the expectations of the institution and eventually becomes the very manifestation of prisoner. The new recruit in the military will also adapt and begin to manifest the reactions and adjustments to the expectations of the army in order to assume the role of a military person.

With regards to the mental institution, Goffman's observations led him to believe that patients who are labeled or viewed as mentally ill will be treated as if all their behaviors are manifestations of assumed disorders. One would expect, therefore, that a patient who resists maltreatment by a guard will be viewed in terms of her/his disorder, and not that maltreatment provoked the patient's angry response.

Let us return to the initial skepticism about psychotherapists and the profession in general. The client is not altogether wrong that there is something to worry about. The client has the right to be skeptical when even a part of the perception feared is the one that's true.

How then can the client place trust in the therapist? How does a therapist decide that a client is cured from an illness once a diagnosis has been made? Does a therapist ever not label a client? Once diagnosed as disordered, can an individual emerge from the label as mentally healthy and without residual stigma?

Moreover, what diagnostic tools are in place to measure the progress toward mental health? How does the client know the therapist is right in his assessment? If a client wakes up in the morning and begins to feel better, is his behavior markedly un-disordered?

What kind of oversight needs to be employed when it becomes obvious that the therapist's lenses are tainted with label residue? Professional bias is likely to add to the client's difficulties, and over time, increase the likelihood that the client's dysfunction will increase, not decrease.

There is essentially little incentive to examine or monitor the quality of services received. Once a psychotherapist becomes licensed, it can be assumed that no one questions the opinions, treatment plans or diagnoses of clients. Paperwork is regularly submitted to insurance companies with only the diagnoses and treatment plan as evidence that a client is being served, not that the client receives quality care.

3

The Therapist Always Knows Best

The goals of a perfect therapeutic alliance would begin with "starting where the client is." However, the flip side of today's therapeutic alliance is designed to benefit the therapist more than it is the client.

You cannot have a relationship in which one person is the expert and the other desiring of help without an exchange of power taking place. One is the expert, strong and paternalistic, the other acknowledges his own weakness or inadequacy at solving a particular problem.

The goal of the therapeutic relationship is arguably ethical, but it also runs the danger of fostering dependence in the client. Because it is the role of the therapist to assert one's expertise into a crisis situation in such a convincing fashion, the client often feels a false sense of trust in the therapist's abilities to provide care. As long as the client comes back, the therapist is re-assured of the validity of the treatment plan and the client's desire to be absolved from the pain. Fostering dependency is not an advantage for the client.

Acknowledging vulnerabilities can be a painful and dis-empowering experience. The agreement between the two is based on an assumption that the therapist knows what is best for the client. For the morally challenged therapist, it is sometimes possible to sap a client's essential strength and vitality in order to resolve the therapist's own issues or to make money. The suspicion surrounding the idea of the immoral therapist is born out.

It is unlikely that a client who buys into what the therapist is saying is prepared to defend against the confusion over professional boundaries. "Do no harm" ethics cannot help this sorry situation. The client has a right to be suspicious of the goals of therapy. With little oversight, it is unlikely that it will become apparent that the therapist may have a raging Axis I or II disorder.

Do therapists assess their own mental health when dealing with clients? Who is to say that therapists do not project onto their clients the symptoms that they do not see in themselves? Even in a small community, if a therapist develops a reputation among other therapists as engaging in unethical practices, it is likely that consumers will remain in the dark. If a scandal develops, there is little incentive for community professionals to report such incidents to a responsible authority lest they bring unwanted attention to their own practices.

One professional put it this way: "Immoral and illegal things happen all the time in organizations around this community; it's just become expected as part of business." Of course, no one is talking about the harm caused to the consumer. Certainly no one remembers their "do no harm" ethic[1, 2] at a time when their own professional image is at stake.

4

What We Mean by Mental Health

Psychotherapists differ in their opinions about what constitutes average mental health. However, there is no agreement or uniformity about which behaviors, thoughts or emotions we can consider to be adaptive, mentally healthy and developmentally appropriate for each of our clients.

Psychotherapy can be viewed as a subjective science. In no other discipline can the observer become an expert on the deviant behavior or deviant mental health in a relatively unknown person after only a few sessions with a client. In no other field can a client be diagnosed with a condition in which the label can be more debilitating than the actual condition.

Therapists operate as if they are able to distinguish mental health from unhealth through observation of the client's behavior during the interview process. One glimmer of the client's total universe and the small window of opportunity turns into a large panorama of maladaptive behaviors.

Usually by the fourth visit (in fact about three hours of total time with the client) the diagnosis is made with treatment goals and objectives aligned with diagnostic criteria from the DSMMD. Therapists who are uncertain about a client's symptoms might defer for three sessions before a diagnosis is made. However, there is still ongoing pressure to come up with a diagnosis by the fourth visit in order to appease insurance standards for reimbursement of services. Even more astounding, Medicare regulations require therapists to send in their diagnoses upon the first visit.

By achieving the goals of therapy, it is the hope of every therapist that the client will eventually generalize newly learned adaptive behaviors to other realms of the client's life. To be able to achieve this generalization, the client must be mentally competent and able to learn easily, function more adaptively, and be able to work through narrowly defined guidelines provided by the psychotherapist. This approach also assumes that such objectives match the nature and severity of the client's dysfunction. Are the goals of treatment achievable by the client? How will the client know when he or she has achieved the objectives? Must the client unlearn certain behaviors in order to acquire new ones?

A therapist must also be a teacher. The answers to good therapy may lie in identifying for the client those behaviors that debilitate the client's functioning in the real world. The therapy room however is not the real world. The client is unable to demonstrate interaction with the real world. How then will the therapist know that the client knows how to correct maladaptive behaviors?

It raises the question of who decides what are maladaptive behaviors for the client and when they have stopped. Unfortunately, looking at a client through the lenses of pathology, all maladaptive behaviors are seen as mental illness. With this interpretation of the individual, it makes it difficult to discern what mental health or normal behaviors look like in the client.

What should be happening to make goals more achievable? Assessing accurately the purpose of behaviors in the individual is critical to finding appropriate goals of intervention with the client. Such an assessment of the individual should include how each client adapts within a variety of social contexts. Viewing the individual as one who is shaped both by unique temperament and a series of experiences is helpful in order to get an accurate understanding of observable behaviors.

Secondly, the therapist can decide if behaviors serve a function, whether they are advantageous or need to be modified to assist in getting from the environment what the client needs. The role of the therapist should be to assist the client in achieving more functional patterns of everyday living, rather than exclusively fixating on pathology. The idea of maladaptive behaviors defining the whole person and the person's experience of the world can sometimes be taken so literally that we forget that the person's behavior is often shaped by the external world. The boundaries between normal and abnormal reactions to experience are blurred.

Should we be diagnosing individuals who have experienced trauma as having a disorder? What do we know about the human psyche when it is exposed, for example, to excessive crimes of war? Individuals who experience symptoms after witnessing a traumatic event may be labeled as having post-traumatic stress disorder.[1] Is it necessary to label something that perhaps is a normal phenomenon of the human condition? This makes little sense when it is already known that the person has been exposed to trauma, and that the symptoms are not endemic to the individual. It is also known that the condition interferes with the individual's ability to cope with life demands. Labeling the individual gives little understanding of how to go about assisting the client with new approaches to life.

Regardless of professional orientation and how certain conditions might be diagnosed, the medical model has influenced psychotherapists and overshadowed the most salient aspects of psychotherapy.

5

The Medical Model

No discussion about the influence of the DSMMD on the mental health profession is complete without talking about the medical model. The medical model was originally a useful approach to human health. For every ailment or disease there is a possible cure or treatment approach. The person must become mentally or physically healthy through the act of curing what is diseased.

Like a bad fungus, the medical model approach grew out of our hospitals and into our homes, professions and employment settings to become insidiously entrenched in our psyches. What started out as a focus in medicine has led to a medical paradigm that has been replicated in every professional milieu related to curing what ails humans. We need to look no farther than prime time television to see its broadest impact. During commercial breaks, we are continually urged to take the right pills for depression, high cholesterol, aching muscles, deteriorating joints or the common cold, that are, of course, "doctor approved." It is easy to see how the medical model approach has had a mesmerizing effect on this culture.

The medical approach opened the doorway for psychiatry and gradually the field of psychotherapy was born. Since the jump to "head doctors," psychotherapists have gradually evolved under the medical model whereby they parallel the position of doctor in a traditional medical setting, define their practice as treating their patients, and continue the assumption that they are healing or curing their patients of some disease or disorder.

Unfortunately, the medical model approach is not easily transferable to psychotherapy. The nasty aftertaste of this approach has left psychotherapy suffering in its identity and place in history as a science to be taken seriously. Following the medical model has resulted in the development of a demeaning attitude toward human frailty, a false set of assumptions about the goals of treatment, and questionable ethics about what is achievable in therapeutic practice. There are significant differences that make it difficult for the medical field and the mental health field to be joined as partners. The rationale behind carrying out what is essentially a medical treatment approach does not fit with the nature of the psychotherapeutic alliance.

If therapists are supposed to be like medical doctors, it can be assumed that a cure must be on the way. Thus, treatment plans would reflect achievable results, with the client cured of the disorder. But is a mentally disordered client ever cured? How can anyone know this to be true?

If the psychotherapist assumes the role of medical doctor of human behavior, then the therapist should set out to snuff out the disease, to eradicate the dysfunction in clients by using effective medications. This has been an inevitable and unfortunate turn in the road in some professional camps. If the medication is effective, the psychotherapist should assume that the client's condition is cured, that the symptoms have dissipated and the client is relieved of suffering. It should also be assumed that the pill will end the need for the person to return to therapy in the future.

Why then is psychotherapy needed at all? Because of the belief that psychotherapists have generated about their cause: that clients are more than their disease, are capable of self-evaluation, and possess the ability to heal themselves. What makes psychotherapy different from the medical counterpart is the belief that the human psyche is dynamic and that healing can occur regardless of the pill one takes. It is ironic that the worthy professional stance on human interaction has had to suffer an identity crisis just because psychotherapists have adopted a medical treatment approach. This orientation does not suit our cause.

Diagnosing what is pathological or abnormal and deciding upon a method of fixing anything about the client is where the whole thing goes awry. What can be said about mental health is that no one is cured of anything. In fact, the ultimate myth is that we have the power to cure mental illness in others.

Even if clients were to be given a quick fix pill that would lessen the symptoms of schizophrenia, the client is not cured. Pills can improve the quality of the human experience but little more. There is no such thing as curing the disease in a client. Perhaps it is time for psychotherapists to rally behind the notion that doing psychotherapy is all about dealing with people who have dysfunctional life patterns.

With the exception of individuals who must operate within an institutional framework, beyond most psychotherapeutic efforts, individuals may be viewed as ranging on a continuum in life skills, some more accustomed to life challenges than others.

Social workers have a professional orientation of looking at the person in the environment or what has been termed, ecological perspective. The individual's difficulties are viewed as part of a larger social context and not at all consistent with the premise that the person is the pathology.

The idea that people are in some way both active contributors and receivers in life situations is a clue to therapists about what really matters to the consumer: that working with levels of functionality may be more important than identifying a disorder. Curing, even in the best sense of helping people, has nothing to do with mending the human spirit and making people more adept at handling their immediate life challenges. In short, psychotherapists need to acknowledge what is curable from what is not, to recognize that consumers are looking for a service that will focus on providing the essential tools to affect new change and more functionality in their lives.

The difference in perspective needs to start with the therapist. If individuals are viewed as having the ability to affect change and their difficulties interfacing with the world around them are viewed in practical terms, therapists may need to recognize their role may also change to that of teacher.

Teaching the client to become more functional may mean understanding which behavioral patterns need to change, and introducing alternative behaviors that coincide with the consumer's best interests, aptitudes, abilities, and strengths. Viewing the client as a choice maker, rather than one who avoids responsibility, may help a client to set standards to follow to a more fulfilling way of life.

Being clearer about which limitations actually exist will set boundaries for clients to work within their own realm of possibilities. If the goals of intervention are clear, the client should be able to recognize success, the surest way of knowing that patterns will be generalized to other areas of the person's life.

Up until now, because the medical model has been so widely implemented, it is difficult for therapists to recognize other approaches that might be more useful. Shifting away from the medical model can be done in such a way that the therapist can incorporate what is worthwhile about the DSMMD when serious mental illness is in question, but also be able to use other diagnostic approaches, as well as assessment instruments, when the problem lies elsewhere, for example, loss of a job.

The International Classification of Functionality, Disability and Health (ICF)[1] is an alternative descriptive approach that provides a focus on a client's specific situation and functionality. We will explore the use of this model in a later chapter.

Clinicians of course will need to work on their own professional images

as they relinquish the magician's robes and eliminate the need to patholo-
gize every person that is contacted. The DSMMD five axis diagnosis has rel-
evance when applied to serious mental illness. Too many of the problems
that clients bring to psychotherapists, however, require a different approach.
For example, a marital difficulty need not require that the therapist try to
find an identified patient when there is none. If therapists are astute, their
treatment plans might become more practical and measurable and there
may be less of a need to worry about their own accountability.

The issue of accountability will be addressed in the next chapter, as
well as the professional ethics involved with business transactions without
consumer awareness or informed consent.

6

The World of Secrecy

It is part of the world of therapists to diagnose clients and submit their diagnostic labels to governmental and organizational entities without the informed consent of their clients. This process has become a gateway for other violations of consumer confidentiality. The secrecy surrounding diagnoses and money exchange is an ethical issue facing today's therapist. Abuse of such a process can occur, but even this is little known to most clients.

No one will dispute that most professionals have a desire to help persons in crisis and that this has always been the primary motive behind providing therapy to clients. Yet, there are clear indications that beneath the fringe of the trade, there is actually more of a business relationship that exists, which may come at a cost to the client. An exchange of power will change the dynamics of the therapeutic relationship permanently. Without the client's awareness or informed consent, a diagnosis will be made by a therapist to be furnished to the health insurance program which will decide whether to pay for therapy sessions.

The client enters the therapeutic relationship wanting help from the therapist yet is unsure as to what the actual service entails. The therapist is under no illusion of the services for sale: a diagnostic label and a treatment plan for a fee. The primary focus is kept on the client in crisis, not the exchange of money or power. Little is said or settled about services as a business transaction.

If the client is eligible for a health insurance program to pay for services, there may be no awareness that a business transaction is going on in the client's behalf. Beyond the scope of the therapeutic alliance, the client will not be aware of what actually lies at the bottom of the well.

The passage of the Health Insurance Portability and Accountability Act of 2003 (HIPPA)[1] requires all medical and mental health organizations and entities to provide the privacy rules to consumers. Consumers are asked to sign a consent form to indicate that they have been informed of what the rules contain.

Here is where the trick of it lies. It really does not mean that there is confidentiality regarding the consumer's records. The form does not address consumers' rights to privacy. It actually means that the consumer is being informed of all the various ways in which consumer information can be used by the organizations or entities without additional consumer consent.

Readers should review the details of the consent form they were last asked to sign when visiting any health professional, to ascertain the extent to which their information may be shared without further consent.

The important message is that the private health information of any consumer can be transmitted for the use of the organization. HIPPA is not designed for the protection of the consumer, but for the protection of the organization from liability claims.

What is even more disconcerting where consumer rights are concerned is that the recent passage of a federal law broadens the world of secrecy and further compromises consumer confidentiality. In the *National Association for Social Workers, California News*, dated July 2004.[2] Mr. Milton Kalish reveals to us that Section 215 of the USA Patriot Act[3] states that the Department of Justice can obtain a court order requiring the release of clinical records without showing cause, and therapists are forbidden to disclose that their client's records have been seized under penalty of law, including possible incarceration.

Mr. Kalish goes on to say that "even though the principle of confidentiality may be at risk, to date, no professional association has addressed this matter in a meaningful manner." He also adds that Section 215 "allows the government access to our confidential clinical records and provides no safeguards as to how the information will be used. From a practical perspective, psychotherapists are now faced with ethical dilemmas. One dilemma is whether or not psychotherapists should tell clients about the possible breach of confidentiality. Simply knowing that this law exists could interfere with the capacity of some clients to trust the clinical relationship, especially those who do not trust the government. By not telling the client, however, the psychotherapist may become uneasy about providing treatment under false pretenses and the failure to fulfill the ethical mandate."

This constitutes another potential abuse of the consumer's rights over their own confidential records and seemingly, both the consumer and psychotherapist have no control over the situation. The only possible ethical posture for a psychotherapist may be to inform clients in advance that without their knowledge or consent their confidential information could be disclosed. The same may be said when an agency requires the disclosure of confidential information to a third party payer in order to receive reimbursement for services. A case example in a publication for social workers addresses this specific issue.[4]

Why should the client care as long as the service is provided? Because the client has no direct knowledge that he has given away his privacy rights or power to decide the range of services. He understands even less that he has been given a devastating label in order to justify the need for continued service.

There are consequences for acquiring a diagnostic label that may not, in the end, benefit the client. Rather, everyone except the client may be profiting off of the back of the client's frailties or inadequacies.

Most clients are unaware that as a part of the business transaction, an assessment generally follows with a diagnosis of the client's overall mental health status.

The client is not brought into the process by the therapist unless the client is deemed to have insight into the disorder.[5] Being at the weakest point of psychological strength, the consumer is not going to be in the mental framework to evaluate the quality of the services or to care much about what is happening behind the scenes. From behind the scenes, the paperwork and the labeling going on is doing anything but helping the client.

In the world where labeling prevails and HMOs rule, the consumer is at risk for receiving a debilitating diagnosis, via DSMMD. On paper, the client may have contracted a rare disorder that, unannounced to him or her, will never heal. Strictly in terms of consumer rights, the client deserves to know that the therapist will be diagnosing the individual and that the label is necessary in order to receive payment for services.

A difficult or resistant client may be explained by one therapist to another as "being the part," in other words, behavior explainable by the disorder. The meta-message shared among therapists when they review their clients over coffee sometimes conveys a bias, for example, the client is a bi-polar person as if that label explains the client's disagreeable attitude. The client never outlives his label because it serves a purpose.

The incentive to follow the procedures outlined by health insurance programs is high, since the DSMMD can be utilized so easily and is valued by the larger systems because it simplifies and categorizes human behavior. This process makes a "difficult people" business into a quantifiable money producing industry.

The problem is that no single entity is verifying the accountability of the verifier. The clients are left out of the business transaction entirely. As discussed earlier, any label can be made to stick if the psychotherapist has a license to practice. When a therapist submits the form indicating a DSMMD diagnosis to an insurance company, it is assumed that the label and treatment goals are appropriate to the consumer's need for the professional's services.

Clients eligible for Medi-Cal in California may receive psychotherapy with no responsibility for co-payment for therapeutic services. Every psychotherapist knows that in return for the most severe of diagnoses on a particular client, financial compensation will follow for every session in which face to face contact with the client has been made.

The most gratifying aspects of this arrangement from the point of view of the psychotherapists are the freedoms that come with controlling how their paperwork will look to the third party payer and the power that comes from professional decision-making.

A psychotherapist may receive referrals from an agency and be able to choose which ones to keep and which ones to pass on to other therapists. What psychotherapists have lost in the pressures to comply with eligibility criteria is some of their own abilities to control service outcome and see the progress in their clients.

Unfortunately, no one is examining exactly how decisions are reached, nor who has been helped or hurt by the process. Certainly, clients are kept in the dark unless they request a look at the therapists' reports. Services to the consumer may be more than were bargained for in the business transaction with the therapist. Will the client as consumer consider this a bargain deal if other important people in the client's world were to see the report (for example, the person's employer)?

Would the client consider this to be a helping relationship if the ramifications of behind the scenes business transactions were known? Would anyone prefer to be labeled a bi-polar person as if that defined to others everything one did?

The therapist may be fully convinced that the client is served best through the mental health process. One of the most damaging outgrowths of this system is that the client begins to walk down a never-ending trail of non-recovery.

Therapists are put in the position of adhering to the system instead of ethical practices. Clients may continue to endure an uncomfortable burden of having been labeled with a disorder that remains in their records permanently without their awareness and long after therapy has been terminated.

To add to the confusion of what constitutes a worthy diagnosis in the eyes of the third party payer, individuals who come to a therapist having known disabilities (either physical or cognitive) are flushed through the mental health system as if their disabilities had become mental disorders overnight. For example, it is not so unusual that an individual in a wheelchair who expresses his anger to a social service system entity about the lack of accessibility to public buildings or the inability to get SSI is regarded as a person in need of therapy.

After having been told that he needs to see a therapist because of his anger, the individual arrives at the doorstep of the therapist still angry about the whole situation and proceeds to describe how unfairly he has been treated thus far. He is then told by the therapist, "You are just angry about being disabled; let's work on some of that anger," rather than recognizing that the client is angry because of the lack of access to public buildings, the fact that he was rejected for SSI, or insulted by the social services worker who stated that he needed therapy.

On paper to the insurance company, the psychotherapist is inclined to diagnose the individual as having some sort of serious disorder, for example, clinical depression or suffering from an anxiety disorder NOS (not otherwise specified). The diagnosis has no merit in this situation but it simply becomes a matter of routine to the therapist to send in the new, more debilitating diagnosis on paper to the insurance company so that services will be paid for.

Professional ethics be damned in this situation. Not only does the diagnosis not reflect the individual's primary problem, but now the individual has accrued one more additional problem in his life challenges: that of getting a brand new Axis I disorder.

The differences between disability and disorder are necessary to understanding how to work with clients with their present life challenges. Therefore these differences will be explored in the next chapter along with a discussion about how the DSMMD has made it difficult to assess the needs of this population, and perhaps has inadvertently contributed to many of the negative stereotypes that exist today.

7

Twin Sisters of Different Mothers: Disability or Disorder?

The professional discussion changes here somewhat to the question of who is being assessed and for what reason. In professional circles one can hear the terms disorder and disability used interchangeably, and wonder at the lack of clarity between using each when assessing clients. Should professionals care about this distinction at all? Yes. The terms may be similar but cater to differing contexts.

Imagine that you have suddenly broken your leg. Would you not expect to be treated by medical doctors as if the broken limb was the problem? Instead, you find to your horror that the doctors are not treating your broken leg at all. Rather, they begin treating you as if you are mentally insane because you are screaming in agony.

By another example, you would be equally outraged if a surgeon decided to operate in order to remove a brain tumor on the right side of your brain and by mistake removed a different part of the brain located on the left side. Although this phenomenon is not too common, it does happen.

The answer as to why professionals need to take care to distinguish disability from disorder is contained in the above examples. Confusing the term disability with disorder produces roughly the same type of mistake, and can have profound consequences for a client's future functioning in the world.

Furthermore, if you are paying attention, the reality is that becoming more functional in the world is the primary focus of most clients. It should not be lost due to bad medical or psychological intervention.

In the medical world the goals of treatment surround the need to cure the disease. A disability differs in that individuals who experience impaired function carry limitations into their living situation that resist curing.

Having impaired function means the person's connections to the larger social and ecological framework have changed. The internalization of one's self concept will naturally change as the individual now must absorb social and lifestyle challenges that have not had to be faced before.

Psychotherapists unfamiliar with anything but DSMMD may have difficulties discerning what their role should be to the client who comes to them with an obvious disability. It may be more comfortable for the therapist to view the client in terms of the therapist's own background, in other words, that of having a psychological disorder because assisting the client with functional living issues does not fit into the DSMMD line of thinking.

The client with a disability, in other words, does not fit comfortably into the "identified patient" model since the usual symptoms associated with a disorder do not define the client's problem. Federal law in the form of the Americans with Disabilities Act[1] is clear in defining disability in terms of an impairment interfering with one or more life functions. This would imply that therapists need to attend to the functional limitations of an individual, but the therapist is rarely trained in this approach.

As in the broken leg scenario, if the therapist is not in touch with which problem is actually the one the client is most concerned with, an appropriate intervention will not be achieved and a therapeutic alliance will likely dissolve. As in the scenario of the broken leg, professionals can misinterpret the nature of the problem. If the therapist is unable to figure out how to proceed with a client, and the client lashes out angrily over not being heard, the therapeutic relationship is flawed from the start.

Clients need to be validated for their concerns and not fit into the identified patient model because it is convenient for the therapist to treat them so. A person suffering from a bad back does not wish to hear about a cure all pill for anxiety when he may be focused on being able to function at his job with his new disabling condition.

Stereotypes about the disabled and attitudes on the part of medical doctors unfortunately have added to the belief that disabled people somehow are also mentally disordered and, that the two terms may be used interchangeably.

Co-author Peter Leech has described his encounter with medical doctors and a psychiatrist shortly after he was confined to a wheelchair at age twenty-three because of polio. Peter can remember approaching a psychiatrist to understand his own feelings of loneliness, anger and depression. In response to Peter's questions, the psychiatrist quickly arrived at his conclusions: "Of course you are angry and depressed. Its because you're disabled. I'd be too."

Somehow, this professional misunderstood the nature of the crisis Peter was experiencing in his life. Peter later came to understand that he was angry and depressed because his life had significantly changed overnight, resulting in life challenges that in his words, "no one seemed to get, but everyone wanted me to just accept."

It is not difficult to imagine how therapists can miss out on understanding the disability experience when the focus has been traditionally medical in nature, that of healing and curing the identified patient. However, psychotherapists do have an edge in the therapeutic process with clients because they have none of the responsibilities of curing and all of the advantages of exploring with clients how they can become more functional in their lives.

Disability is an everyday experience. Disability is everyone's experience. No amount of acceptance of a disability will help a client to become more functional in daily life. Especially if the actual problem is not acknowledged by the psychotherapist, or the medical doctor as well.

In truth, humans encounter this as a common experience. It is unusual to go through a lifetime unscathed by disability. Everyone can recall a member or relative in the family who has had a disability, even if such a person only acquired the disability with age. Whatever the biases or fears, disability symbolizes adaptation, not disorder.

Myth II

The DSMMD Applies to Every Client

Introduction: When the DSMMD Just Doesn't Serve

CASE ILLUSTRATION

Ms. Wasser was wondering what she should do. She had been a psychotherapist for many years and now realized for the first time that she had to decide which member of the family she had been seeing should be considered the person with the disorder.

Medicaid had rejected paying for the mental health services she provided to this family in crisis because, as they had told her in a less than sensitive way, "the DSMMD, V codes[1], were unacceptable diagnoses for payment." In order for her services to be paid for, one of the identified patients must have a serious Axis 1 Disorder.

Ms. Wasser was in a quandary about what to do. She had met with the family for several weeks and had written her treatment plans according to what she ethically could do given the nature of the situation.

The family was in crisis and was coming to Ms. Wasser in desperation. Mr. and Mrs. Gentile had been fighting continuously since Mrs. Gentile's mother had arrived to live with them. Gemina Potter (or "Gem" as she was given as a pet name) had arrived the month before after an incident wherein the 85-year-old senior, who lived alone, had set her home on fire.

The family had been apprised of the event in the middle of the night, and had rushed Gem to the hospital for an evaluation of her mental com-

47

petence. The opinion that Gem had some form of dementia surprised them, although the family admitted that she had been found wandering the streets in two prior episodes over the last year.

What to do with Gem was the current focus of the family strife. Their four children ranged in age from twelve years to eighteen, with the oldest getting ready to go to college. The whole family was fighting over finances and over who should be responsible for Gem's care.

Mr. and Mrs. Gentile began to argue constantly about spending the family savings on care for Gem, especially as it seemed she would eventually need long term care in a nursing home. Interfamilial relationships were breaking down and the children's school performance was deteriorating.

How could Ms. Wasser deal with the insurance carrier in a way that would not add more stress or harm to the family? How could she explain to the family that no money had been provided for therapy and they were rejected based on an arbitrary aspect of the DSMMD? They probably had not the least understanding what that meant and now, neither did she.

She vacillated over what to do, inquired of other therapists what she should do. Many thought she should just play by the rules.

Other therapists confessed that they too had been forced to use more severe diagnoses just to be paid, but did them anyway because private pay clients were just too scarce anymore.

Ms. Wasser was in a personal crisis over what to do. Everyone in the family was, in her opinion, mentally healthy. No pathology could explain the family's dilemma and no identified patient emerged that could be used as the reason for all of the difficulties the family was experiencing. The grief, the sadness, the resentfulness, the imposition of dementia on the lifestyles of innocent people weighed heavily on Ms. Wasser's mind.

She called the insurance carrier to discuss the matter further. Over the phone she received a curt, "I'm sorry, ma'am, but the policies and regulations are in place to keep abuse of the system from happening. It will be up to you to follow the rules if you want to be paid for your client services." And, "if you care that much about them, perhaps you should have a sliding fee scale in private pay as an option for these folks."

Ms. Wasser tried to explain that the family could not pay but needed services badly, that they did not fit neatly under the other DSMMD categories, and that it was unethical to place them there if they really belong in the V codes.

The insurance representative paused on the phone, then said, "Ma'am, this is a business. We don't accept V codes. We don't care at our end what the family's situation is, just that there is some serious mental illness going on. Perhaps the family could get a little help from a spiritual counselor instead?" Ms. Wasser drew a breath as she realized that the policies in place were more rigid than she knew. She hung up the phone and despaired over what to do.

A few more weeks went by. Ms. Wasser could not bring herself to send in an Axis 1 Diagnosis. The ethical dilemma as she saw it was whether or not to work for free and ignore her own financial crisis or refer the family on. If she referred the family on, some other therapist could diagnose one of the family members inappropriately. Harm would be inflicted by some other professional onto the family's disadvantaged situation.

Ms. Wasser had many sleepless nights. Finally, she approached the family and explained that she was leaving private practice. When asked why, she explained that she could not in good faith open the family up to more labels, strife, and in the end, unintended harm. The family understood, although they demanded to know how she could desert them in their time of trouble. Ms. Wasser explained the situation briefly, then walked out of the building.

In the days ahead, Ms. Wasser closed her office, sold her home and moved to another county. She is now teaching in a community college.

The Ethics of Professional Decision Making

Obviously, Ms. Wasser was in a dilemma when it came to making a choice to serve her clients. The ethical dilemma was whether to ignore her financial situation and work for free or apply an unethical diagnosis for payment. This would mean, labeling an identified patient in the family with a severe diagnosis that she did not agree with.

Ms. Wasser wanted to make the best ethical decision possible regarding her clients. She concluded that she could not pass them along to another therapist who might go along with the insurance company standards and diagnose one of the family members improperly.

Ms. Wasser's ethical dilemma, however, is not the only ethical dilemma worth mentioning. It is clear that the family's situation does fit within the V codes listed in the DSMMD, but it is also clear that the DSMMD system of diagnosing mental illness does not fit with these types of family situations.

It is unethical to unfairly characterize any family member in the above case scenario as an identified patient. It is also unethical to diagnose any person inappropriately, finding pathology just to adhere to insurance company demands. Furthermore, it has raised questions about the ethics of exposing clients unnecessarily to the labeling process just to fit within the DSMMD system of diagnosing pathology.

To review, the V codes are indicators of life events, environmental factors or stressors (in this case, Gem's progressive dementia) that are viewed as outside influences affecting the mental and behavioral states of clients (in this case, Gem's family members.) To again repeat, insurance companies do not recognize V codes for financial re-imbursement of therapy services. As it stands now, therapists are in the position of placing blindfolds over their eyes, diagnosing a family member as having a disorder and sending this information on to insurance companies in order to be paid.

It is very clear that the responsibility for ethical decision making rides squarely on the head of every practicing therapist. The insurance company is not apt to regard their own practices as contributing to the harm of clients. The insurance company is not likely to think about confidentiality, even though the diagnoses are entered into a large computer network wherein the intimate details about the therapeutic meetings might be available to anyone in the organization to access at whim.

The pressure to fit any person into a diagnosis for the purposes of financial re-imbursement to the therapist is more than just an ethical breach. It betrays the trust of every client and compromises in every sense the "do no harm" principle.

The sad thing is that the DSMMD influence has expanded well beyond its intended use. It was never intended to become an instrument of inclusion or exclusion of people for receipt of social services, or financial reimbursement from insurance companies. The authors of the DSMMD manual also never intended that professionals would engage in unethical practices, using it as the basis of questionable professional judgment.

If there is any blame to be shared in all of this, state licensing boards must be held accountable as the authoritative entities that impose control over the licenses of thousands of helping professionals. The boards are raising a new generation of business professionals, adept in the practice of mental health, who are required to subscribe to professional ethics to the highest esteem.

Roll out the red tape and regulations; these organizations do it all when it comes to licensing the cream of the crop. They are supposed to be the governing body protecting the consumer from abuses of the system. Yet they are curiously silent at taking a stand about how diagnoses should be made and how they should be employed. The mental health industry certainly knows how to make money off the backs of consumers and no one is asking, but what about the ethics and what about protecting consumers?

Nevertheless, it must be said that the authors and publishers of the DSMMD are not immune to receiving their own share of criticism. At some level they must be aware of how diagnoses are made by professionals. They must be aware of how the classifications are used by insurance companies and continue to be a part of social system networks and other governmental entities.

The DSMMD has been allowed to become widespread without any controls imposed on its use and it now appears everywhere globally in every conceivable way. No one is questioning the ethics of the persons that should know better. The sales of the DSMMD bring money to the organization and the empire keeps growing.

Could it be that these professionals are too busy profiting off the backs of consumers to care about the multiple uses of the DSMMD? Or to be concerned with how the consumer is harmed? Or to care about how the DSMMD criteria are being misused, or misapplied in schools, social service networks, and other service organizations across America and around the world?

In the chapters ahead, the role of the DSMMD within the diagnostic process will be examined; how it has been employed and used for its authoritative place in professional practices. Its influence may be seen in some of the most unexpected places, for example, schools, governmental agencies such as the Department of Vocational Rehabilitation etc. Since the DSMMD grew into its own widespread industry it has been revered to the extent that it can be considered an American institution unto itself. From this perspective the reader will begin to understand which populations have been most affected by its use as part of the diagnostic process.

8

Humpty Dumpty's Guide to the DSMMD: Critical Issues in the Diagnostic Approach

When Humpty fell down and broke his crown, no one had the foggiest idea how to help him. And as the old rhyme goes: "All the King's horses and all the King's men could not put Humpty together again." It is unlikely that they had the Diagnostic and Statistical Manual of Mental Disorders (DSMMD)[1] to guide them.

Today the psychotherapist is indeed blessed with a good bed of knowledge about how to classify Humpty's symptoms into diagnostic categories. The DSMMD has made it possible to diagnose his and many other mental conditions so that an approach to treatment can be found, making it possible for Humpty to put all those pieces back together again. This is a book about the ethics of using diagnostic labels and the professional decision making process. This chapter will focus on a brief overview of the DSMMD, describe what it is designed to do, how it is organized and how a diagnosis is formally written on paper in the format commonly referred to as the Five Axis Diagnosis.[2] This basic knowledge of the way the manual is utilized by clinicians for the purpose of diagnosis is essential to understanding later chapters which will describe professional roles and discuss the way clients are directly affected by labeling when it is applied as part of the psychotherapeutic process. The concepts will be explained in simplified terms so that lay readers may understand what is useful to know about the DSMMD. If one looks at the intentions of the authors of the manual in developing this diagnostic reference, one immediately understands that the criteria used for each mental disorder are considered to be "guidelines to be informed by clinical judgment and are not to be used in a cookbook fashion."[3]

Nevertheless, using the DSMMD is much like going to the supermarket in that you know that you have in mind the type of food you might be looking for. But among food items, you want to find just the one that includes the type of ingredients and nutritional value desired. To find it, you read through the labels for size, proportions of servings and nutritional value on the side of the package. Sometimes it is helpful for the psychotherapist to go down each aisle of the larger more complete version of the supermarket, the lengthy DSMMD, or sometimes it is quicker to use the mini-manual desk reference. And, just like a trip to any supermarket, you will open the manual to find lists of disorders with their own specific code numbers which appear under major headings or classifications of types of disorders.

The coding system is derived from the International Classification of Diseases, Ninth revision, Clinical Modification, referred to as ICD-9-CM. The DSMMD (DSM-IV) has a numerical code which precedes the name of the disorder in the classification as well as a description of each disorder named.

There are some diagnostic categories such as mental retardation for which the therapist may need to engage in further investigation of the criteria or symptoms. It is also possible that the client may show symptoms other than those listed in the manual. Because those symptoms may appear concurrently with other grouped symptoms that the therapist deems most salient, the term Not Otherwise Specified or NOS is applied with a separate code.

Specifiers indicate a rating of severity, that is, the intensity of the symptom expressed. Specifiers include: mild, moderate, severe, in partial remission, full Remission, and prior history. The ratings of severity are extremely important for therapists to note because the DSMMD allows for the possibility of recovery. The diagnostic report may include a section that indicates when the individual has indeed recovered. However, records being records, the individual cannot escape the prior history of diagnosis and treatment because this is also indicated on the diagnostic report. Records do not change over time and will remain permanent as evidence that the individual once was given a diagnosis of a mental disorder.

A diagnosis must be based on the person's current symptoms or state of functioning. It is perhaps important here to repeat the fact that conducting an assessment should be always based on the client's current symptoms. This does not always occur however. In practice, the diagnostician may simply be inclined to rely on a previous diagnosis when unsure about the client's symptoms. It should be emphasized that the DSMMD is typically not used to deal with previous diagnoses; that is, as if a diagnosis of a particular disorder is ongoing. If an individual is found to be in full remission, the diagnostician must be aware that the individual has indeed recovered and acknowledge that the previous diagnosis cannot continue to be used. This is an important issue of diagnosis because out in the field, clinical use of the DSMMD may be misapplied or abused if guidelines are overlooked.

Specifiers of mild, moderate, and severe are used only when the full criteria for the disorder are met. The psychotherapist must look at the degree of severity as well as type of symptoms presented to determine whether the individual fits the description of a disorder. Symptoms that might indicate other disorders must be ruled out before a diagnosis is made. However, it is possible that an individual might meet the criteria for more than one disorder.

What often evades the view of the diagnostician who is operating on a "business as usual" basis, is the ethical responsibility that goes along with labeling a client. It is doubtful that the therapist is thinking about the potential harm that could come to the client as the result of imposing a diagnostic label. The creation and general use of the manual itself is not where the root of the criticisms lie but in the misapplication of its criteria to diagnose individuals, and misuse of diagnoses in various social and professional contexts.

As has already been alluded to, diagnostic labels follow clients in the form of permanent records. If one looks at the state of today's health care and legal systems in practice, evidence of abuses can be seen. It is not unusual to find examples of legal court cases in which public figures have been exploited by the media for having sought treatment for a particular problem. The psychiatric histories of the individuals engaged in legal battles are released to the public in a most unfavorable light.

Tipper Gore comes to mind as a public figure who was ostracized and abused for having once sought treatment for depression. The media and politicians had a field day scrutinizing her during her husband's campaign for the presidency. No one probably remembers ever experiencing a depressed moment themselves, but likely they remember Tipper as forever linked with having mental illness. To her credit, she went on later to advocate for the rights of the mentally ill.

In short, the individual is vulnerable to potential abuses that may occur as the result of past diagnoses. Because there is no control over the interpretation of the label in question, an entire career may suffer the consequences of diagnostic labeling. In fact, psychiatric records can surface in civil, criminal or custody issues.

Furthermore, because the manual uses a specifier to indicate that an individual has had a prior history of a disorder, this fact must be recorded in the diagnostic report. Knowing that someone has had a prior history can impact current life situations. For example, some job applications still ask if you have ever been treated for an emotional or mental disorder. Even if the individual submits a copy of the therapist's final report to the employer, indicating that he or she has recovered from a previous diagnosis, the specifier of prior history could shatter the person's chances of being hired.

Again the issue of ethics and sound professional decision making on the part of psychotherapists comes into play. It is possible that the client may be able to move on with life free from anxiety, or the symptoms of a particular disorder, but in an imperfect world the label remains fixed. The client is never free from suspicion, future labeling of past behavior, or free from public scrutiny for having sought help for a particular problem.

Few people escape the ostracism and the stigma of having been labeled as mentally ill, even if this interpretation is false, or the individual is considered fully recovered. In other words, once disordered, always disordered in the court of public opinion.

Erving Goffman makes the point that among the three different types of stigma, "There are blemishes of individual character perceived as weak will, domineering or unnatural passions, treacherous and rigid beliefs, and dishonesty, these being inferred from a known record of, for example, mental disorder, imprisonment, addiction, alcoholism, homosexuality, unemployment, suicidal attempts and radical political behavior."[4] Most mental health professionals would not equate diagnostic labeling with Erving Goffman's definition of stigma. Yet, the aftermath of the great DSMMD revolution has produced a kind of relaxed professional climate around the use of diagnostic labeling with every client. With the gradual acceptance of diagnostic labels within the mental health arena, a general acceptance has also grown of its use within institutional frameworks. Diagnostic labels have become in effect "stigmatizing labels"[5] in the lives of many unknowing, often disenfranchised clients for the purposes of social compliance, efficiency of human service delivery and profit.

Reviewing the Five Axis Diagnosis

The diagnosis is written using a five axis format which will not be shown here. The interested reader can quickly find the Five Axis Diagnosis format on page 25 of the DSM-IV.[6] The reader will find below a brief description of the criteria used under each axis.

Axis I is used to report mental disorders that are usually considered chronic. Axis I does not include those disorders referred to as personality disorders or mental retardation. Personality disorders and mental retardation are noted on Axis II.

Axis II can also be used to note maladaptive personality features and commonly used defense mechanisms. Personality disorders are diagnosed on the basis of how symptoms are manifested over time, regarded by psychotherapists as severe, and are difficult to address with psychotherapy. What is perhaps noteworthy to mention is that clients diagnosed with personality disorders or mental retardation are not generally served by insurance companies. The reason is perhaps that both problems are seen as permanent and non-recoverable.

To meet the criteria for diagnosis of mental retardation, the IQ of an individual must be determined to be at least 70 or below. Individuals must also have concurrent deficits in adaptive functioning expressed in at least two of the following areas: communication, self-care, home living, social interpersonal skills, self-direction, functional academic skills, work, leisure, health and safety. The onset for mental retardation must be before eighteen years of age.

Axis III is used to report current medical conditions that may be relevant to understanding and treating the individual's mental disorder—for example, disorder as residual from heart or head injury, etc.

Axis IV is used to report psychosocial and environmental problems considered to be stressors or adverse life events for the individual. Stressors may affect the diagnosis, treatment, and prognosis for mental disorders. In other words, the mental state or behavior is viewed as residual from external life conditions, e.g. poverty, domestic abuse conditions, etc. Insurance companies typically will not pay for psychotherapy when a client has a diagnosis on Axis IV (for example, adjustment disorder).

Axis V is used to report the clinician's assessment of the individual's global level of functioning. Using the Global Assessment of Functioning Scale that is included in the DSMMD, the diagnostician can consider psychological, social and occupational functioning on a continuum of severity to determine the level of mental health or illness. A number system is used to indicate the level of severity of the individual's disorder. The DSMMD is clear about the fact that the severity of the impairment may not be caused by physical or environmental factors. It should be noted that, on the scale of Global Assessment, a score of 50 or below will enable a client to receive therapy paid for by insurance companies. A disorder considered this severe must also contain behavioral symptoms that impact the individual in at least one of the following areas of functioning: impact in a job setting, impact in a school setting, or the ability to establish social connections with the outside world (this may pertain to an individual who is either seen as suicidal or delusional).

According to the DSM-IV, most psychosocial problems will be indicated on Axis IV. However when a psychosocial problem such as the death of a loved one or loss of a job becomes the central focus of therapy, such environmental problems should be marked in Axis I under a section entitled Other Conditions (see above). Other psychosocial problems may include difficulties with primary support group, problems related to the social environment, education problems, access to social systems, or legal issues.

Although the DSMMD does take into account environmental factors and the degree of functionality, these issues are not adequately addressed when considering a treatment direction. There are other effective tools which may better focus on how the individual interacts or interfaces with the immediate social environment.

Other difficulties arise with the use of the DSMMD that adversely affect persons applying for social services or psychotherapy. As we have indicated above, not all diagnoses (especially those on Axis II and IV) get the benefits of services paid for through insurance programs.

Societal issues also impact individual behavior and create emotional duress, for example, minority oppression. It would be difficult to assess a social problem such as racial hatred in terms of the DSMMD.

Consider racial unrest in the south during the 1960s. The impact of growing up in a hostile environment might produce in the individual a set of behaviors based on the cultural expectations of the times. If the individual were to lash out at the hypocrisy and prejudice, he or she would be seen exclusively in terms of that behavior resulting from mental illness and not that there was any sort of relationship between the individual and the racist chain of events.

The manual also introduces what are known as V codes.[7] V codes are used to categorize those situations in therapy when it is clear that a pattern of interaction may cause symptoms in one person or more. For example, in the case of a divorce, spouses may be characterized as exhibiting negative communication behaviors. The DSMMD would regard symptoms that arise for either individual reacting to the event negatively as the center and focus of psychotherapy. Thus, this type of therapeutic focus would be categorized under V codes.

The unfortunate aspect of being categorized under V codes is that insurance companies have not wanted to pay for and have rejected therapy services in which the focus is based in part on life circumstances (for example, divorce) and not on problems considered endemic to the individual. Other life situations that clients face that are categorized under V codes in the manual include: relational problems when related to a medical condition, parent-child relationships, sibling relational problems and those problems that may be considered relational problems NOS. V codes may also include those issues considered related to abuse and neglect, physical or sexual abuse of an adult, anti-social or non-compliant behavior in children and adolescents, and borderline intellectual functioning.

It should be emphasized that the DSMMD is a very useful and complete manual for identifying and diagnosing serious and persistent mental illness. However, when regarding the continuum of factors affecting and influencing human behavior that fall outside the scope of serious and persistent mental illness, the DSMMD lessens in shine and narrows considerably in its accuracy.

The next few chapters will focus on the ethics involved with using the DSMMD in the practice of psychotherapy and examine more closely what is meant by therapeutic alliance. The loss of consumer confidentiality due to the involvement of third party payers will also be addressed.

9

About Fitting the Square Peg into the Round Hole

The responsible psychotherapist today naturally utilizes the DSMMD to come up with some diagnosis that captures the essence of the client's problem. But does the DSMMD always offer the essence of the client's problem?

Are there times when the diagnostic tool could be thrown out with the bath water? People of cultural diversity may or may not fit into this picture easily. The differences of language, cultural traditions and familial perspectives may not be taken into account by the psychotherapist who is using the DSMMD for diagnostic purposes.

People with disabilities who have never been identified as having mental illness confront many unpleasant, or downright hostile, interactions with their immediate social environment. The individual may have to endure or survive in many oppressive and societal prohibitive situations that the professional can not understand or has no parallel in experience. These experiences may shape the individual's self-perception.

When an individual can not access a restaurant, library or movie theater because of using a wheelchair and the building is inaccessible, the individual is likely to develop a lot of feelings surrounding these negative experiences.

A therapist must be able to look beyond the scope of the DSMMD to see the individual in the context of everyday life. It is an ethical if not a moral responsibility to understand the real life issues of persons who come from different social, educational or cultural backgrounds.

The DSMMD has questionable validity, for example, when it is viewed in term of clients from different cultural backgrounds, from around the world, and their individual frameworks in the contexts of culture and language. Mental health providers cannot continue to study and practice the white, middle class methodology for which many in past years were prepared in graduate studies as if this is the natural way to think about all clients.

The DSMMD reveals more and more its limitations as the world becomes more inevitably non-white. In short, the DSMMD has become an institution outdated by the times.

If therapists are willing to look at an individual within the larger social context, they may realize immediately that therapy is process more than treatment for a particular disorder. In other words, viewing persons as depressed because of the social injustice or oppression they are experiencing is more important than trying to find labels that fit the clients.

More often than not, the public's lives are touched by an individual whose primary challenge has been trying to survive within a chasm of social systems and who is experiencing system induced trauma, a concept that will be addressed in a later chapter.

When the client suffers because of the narrow way the therapeutic process is defined, no one benefits, no one wins, no one receives a roadway to success. When psychotherapists fail to see the inadequacies of using the DSMMD tool exclusively in their practices, the end result may be narrowing the view of our client's world.

As one graduate school professor was fond of saying, "If we take one unflattering view of ourselves, yelling in anger or carrying on in an embarrassing way, and freeze it, is that what we would want others to be focused on about us and make assumptions based on our behaviors?" She has a point.

This is just how people with mental illness are often viewed: without dimensionality outside of their pathological behaviors. People are much more dimensional than their psychiatric labels. They live completely separate lives from therapists who have only a brief period of time to acquaint themselves with the individual and then prescribe a treatment plan.

But it goes further than even this. Even those with obvious diagnoses of serious mental illness should be regarded as more similar than dissimilar to those without mental challenges. There are many more living challenges and everyday experiences that may shape the person's behaviors.

In most respects people who are capable of living independent lives must be considered more functional than they are dysfunctional because they survive. Therefore, shouldn't the goals of therapy be re-addressed to focus on how individuals function within various social contexts rather than be focused simply on the type of illness they have?

The DSMMD cannot present a dimensional view of a client's life. As we have stated already, it was only supposed to group symptoms that commonly appear together into identifiable categories that would assist the therapist in setting priorities for treatment plans.

10

Looking Deeper into the Pond: Continuing the Case Against Diagnostic Labeling

There are some categories that appear in the DSMMD that really do not belong under the classification of mental disorder, for example, invisible disabilities, such as learning disabilities (LD) or attention deficit disorder (ADD).[1, 2]

Nothing can be gleaned from the definitions in DSMMD that would be useful to developing a treatment plan for a person with dyslexia, because essentially no therapy can help someone read the printed word. It can be argued that learning disabilities and attention deficit disorder are essentially disability-based conditions. The individual is born with a natural physiological pre-disposition or trait, much like hair or eye color, which when manifested in exclusive social contexts (for example, learning environments) is recognized as impaired functioning.

Each year, a large number of children and adults worldwide are diagnosed with LD. Depending upon the type of professional doing the diagnosis, the condition is identified either as a disability or as a mental disorder.

For clinical psychologists, the DSMMD provides four categories of learning disorders: reading disorder, mathematic disorder, disorder of written expression, and learning disorder NOS (315.0, 315.1, 315.2, 315.9 DSMMD.)[3]

For school psychologists, the primary method for assessment of learning disabilities has been to use standardized tests of intelligence in conjunction with performance based tests.[4, 5] In some professional camps, learning disabilities have been referred to as information processing disabilities. The DSMMD label and number categories have become a mere formality for the diagnostician to put on the diagnostic report. Very few school psychologists would insist that the DSMMD provides useful information beyond minimal descriptive purposes.

Many psychotherapists in private practice are only vaguely aware of who is providing what in the way of assessments for children and adults suspected of having learning disabilities or attention deficit disorder. Although there is overlap in the field between clinical psychologists, school psychologists, and neuro–psychologists, there is a gap that emerges when attention deficit disorder is introduced into the fold of the conversation.

Attention deficit disorder may be identified by any the above professionals but the diagnosis must be confirmed by a licensed medical doctor, because medications must be involved. If the client responds well to medication, the physician will confirm a diagnosis for ADD.

Ironic, however, is the consensus in the medical community that there are no proven effective drugs that clearly work with all adults having ADD. Some consumers respond to medications, others don't. It is fascinating to learn that there are no clear reasons why certain drugs are chosen over others, other than physician's preference. No one seems to be discussing the real issue at hand: the physicians are good at prescribing medications, the insurance programs are good at paying for them.

Sometimes medications don't work, even with adults who have had a long standing diagnosis of ADD since childhood. When the drug of choice no longer works, the adult is left to search until finding something to fill in for the former drug.

To add to the whole confusing diagnostic affair, one usually does not see a situation in which physicians reversed the diagnosis of ADD. Some physicians are uncomfortable with the idea of adults having ADD in the first place.

There has been controversy surrounding attention deficit disorder leaving some physicians not wanting to diagnose the condition at all. Although there have been efforts at improving the diagnosis with blood work, genetic histories taken from families, and so on, there remains a pervasive uncertainty in the diagnostic arena.

Some professionals say that they believe the child grows out of the condition if the child, now an adult, no longer presents with hyperactivity as one of the symptoms. Seldom however does one see individuals who were diagnosed as children with ADD that "grew out of the issues of ADD" simply because they learned to regulate their own hyperactivity as adults. Behaviors such as inability to sleep, concentrate, regulate mood swings, screen out distractions, attend long enough to follow through with activities, and becoming psychologically overwhelmed under pressure to perform still are prominent and center stage in the life of a person with ADD at any age.[6]

It is dismaying to observe the process of diagnosing ADD. The physician who prescribes anti-depressants for a person suspected of having ADD raises the bar of confusion to a new level. How does the physician know whether he is treating ADD or depression?

Co-author Kristie Madsen asked the above question to a neurologist to see what the answer might be for clarity's sake. The neurologist answered, "Does it matter?" Kristie stated, "Of course, when you consider what the person has endured and what physiological mayhem will be in store when they begin to experience side effects of the drugs they are trying out." The neurologist sighed, looked past Kristie and responded in a matter of fact tone of voice: "If a client came to me to get drug therapy that will help him to do more in his personal life, I give him the drug knowing that it is his choice."

How We Respond to ADD

Attention deficit disorder and learning disabilities are often confused or not understood well by teachers, staff or administrators. Children are treated as if the two descriptions mean the same thing in the classroom. The water gets very murky indeed when those who have been diagnosed with learning disabilities are additionally identified as having ADD.

Behavior problems surfacing constantly signal that there may be trouble ahead for the child who can not conform. Naturally, children will experience a high level of frustration, anxiety and anger when they try to respond to rigid class standards and academic expectations with which they may not be able to compete.

It is important once again to draw a distinction between having a disability and having a mental disorder defined under DSMMD. The controversy that still exists over the origins of learning disabilities will continue to go on even as the numbers of children diagnosed with LD increases.

It is time for the various professional groups to decide that they will deal with the disability arena head on and incorporate current methods to assist with learning skills, or improve a particular student's chances with the use of reading and writing technology.

None of the people having these particular disabilities have ever spoken about the importance of curing themselves with drugs. What seems to stand out among the children and adults alike is that they must live their lives free from being characterized as abnormal by others or it will become the sole pre-occupation of their lives to fight against that characterization.

Furthermore, the professional world must come to terms with the realization that it is unlikely that any person identified as having ADD or LD as a child will outgrow their diagnoses in their lifetimes because they have disabilities from which they cannot recover. Individuals must live their lives with ADD making adjustments at home, the work setting, the school setting and in many cases trying to fit into social milieus where they experience ostracism.

In many cases, sufferers of ADD report having enormous amounts of grief at their lack of social graces. Lack of ability to attend or focus on the important, and impulsive behavior, leads to heartache in trying to hold onto jobs, school, dreams and relationships.[7]

Few therapists have training or experience in what it means for ADD to be a central factor in a marital dispute. When co-author Kristie Madsen worked with college age students having disabilities, she often heard couples say in her office: "What I want is a coach to help me in my personal life and in my marriage with my wife." "No one understands what I have to deal with because my husband has ADD and this ADD thing is sitting there in the middle of my marriage."

One thing is certain in the minds of persons who experience this disability: the living and social issues that accompany the disability are misunderstood. Having a disability means having to deal with life differently at several levels. The therapist who understands this is a rare find.

Living Issues of the Learning Disabled

Unlike the problems of children with ADD, children who experience learning disabilities struggle with invisible limitations that never go away but surface inconsistently depending upon each activity.

Learning disabilities consist of a variety of cognitive and functional limitations unique to the individual. The limitations of a disability may impact the individual in variable ways which are sometimes difficult for even the individual to understand because of the elusive nature of the impairment.[8, 9]

Only when an impenetrable wall goes up in the child's immediate environment (for example, academic expectations, play with peers, etc.) does the child recognize that barriers of learning exist.

Barriers of learning may be more obvious when performance can be compared with same age peers. Functional limitations of disabilities may include any of the following: inability to interpret symbols or symbolic relationships, or to process or integrate conceptual information either visually, auditory or both. Disabilities may be manifested in reading, writing, math, organization, speech and language production, memory and retrieval of information.

Such limitations may overlap with other essential perceptual abilities such as understanding body-in-space relationships, spatial relationships with objects, perceiving social cues accurately and learning to read body language accurately in other people. Understanding the subtleties in language may also be difficult for some people (for example, jokes, puns or other humor-related matter).

Therapists do encounter these individuals on a regular basis whether or not they recognize them as learning disabled. Sometimes these individuals as adults are defined more by their life circumstances. It has already been well documented that a large number of persons with learning disabilities are homeless or housed in prisons.[10]

Even programs designed to deal with the disabled such as the Department of Vocational Rehabilitation do not know quite what to do with the learning disability population. The national (federal and state funded) program has been grossly out of touch with the seriousness and nature of invisible disabilities for years.

The Department of Vocational Rehabilitation provides vocational services to persons with confirmed disabilities. There are a wide range of services to assist clients with getting and maintaining employment once they are diagnosed and meet the eligibility standards. To meet the criteria, people must substantiate their disabling conditions with numerous psychological and medical reports.

For individuals with learning disabilities, standardized tests must have been conducted using intelligence and performance based test instruments. Such reports confirming a diagnosis of specific learning disability are sent to vocational rehabilitation counselors for their review when a client is considered for services.

Tests are conducted usually by a range of psychologists, psychiatrists, medical doctors and other professionals who have proper credentials to do testing for learning disabilities. Tests that are conducted by mental health professionals such as clinical psychologists usually contain a Five Axis Diagnosis based on the DSMMD. These diagnoses and test results are used to determine the nature and severity of a person's disability. The reports tend to show limited information about the functional limitations of a learning disability, may have reduced validity or may even be irrelevant for establishing a vocational impairment. Other difficulties arise when so little is known about how the person is impacted by the disability limitations in social settings.

Those in the vocational rehabilitation system are reliant on professional opinion about the abilities and limitations of each individual because they lack a vocational testing instrument themselves that might reveal how individuals with learning disabilities are limited in work related settings. It has been standard practice in past for counselors to rely so heavily on standardized tests to determine the extent of vocational impairments that they ignore the fact that standardized tests have their own limitations. Decisions may be based entirely on tests whose results are based on the norms of nondisabled individuals.

It may be argued that standardized tests have some validity in the real world, especially with respect to aptitude and basic academic skills such as reading, written language and math. Society does require these skills in order to function economically above the level of picking cabbages or mopping floors. Standardized tests, however, are limited to measuring only a narrow range of performance skills and are inherently culturally biased. They do not reveal the full range of practical skills that might be needed in a vocational setting. Nor do standardized tests tell counselors which job might be a better fit for some one with particular functional limitations. Finally, the tests cannot show how a client with functional limitations may perform in a job setting when needed accommodations or adjustments are provided.

Many jobs require that a client be able to perform duties at a moment's notice. Some of these duties can highlight a person's abilities, assets or strengths. The contrary, however, is also true. The functional limitations of the client's disability may be revealed depending upon the nature or focus of the job. Such functional aspects of jobs may include: the ability to use a phone or interpret accurate phone messages, ability to quickly write spontaneously in a paper-pencil task, the ability to understand job instructions written or oral, the ability to comprehend subject matter or prepare written papers via technology (for example, voice synthesized computer or regular computer system), organize and prioritize job assignments, execute an order on command, use a calculator for specific reasons, follow directions using a map or find a house address by car, the ability to organize and communicate coherently during discussions with one or more persons in a group, the ability to initiate or follow through changes in job duties, the ability to create or use one's ingenuity to problem solve practical dilemmas, ability to work alongside of other people, the ability to perform under pressure, and the ability to regulate one's behavior or adapt within a variety of social settings. Many of these skills fall outside the parameters of what standardized tests are designed to measure.

The goal for the counselor is to determine, along with the client, a vocational avenue which might lead to a specific goal or career position. It is, however, no secret to vocational rehabilitation counselors that the learning disability population is huge, difficult to assess for services, and unlikely to go away any time soon.

Persons with learning disabilities are perplexing to vocational rehabilitation because, on the onehand, persons with LD are considered to be too high functioning to be served as the "severest of the severe." Yet, on the other hand, vocational rehabilitation is aware of the negative reports revealed in the early 1990s that showed that those students identified as learning disabled were not graduating from high school, but dropping out before the ninth grade.[11] Counselors began to address some of the questions in transition team meetings held at the end of high school, aimed at identifying the vocational needs of some students.[12]

Many vocational rehabilitation counselors are reluctant to get involved today with such clients because there is no way of defining what vocational impairment means for this population or establishing a vocational roadway counselors are familiar with.

Vocational rehabilitation counselors are limited in training and education themselves. When it comes to serving persons with learning disabilities who appear to be intellectually average to superior, who perform well below their aptitudes, vocational rehabilitation counselors are at a loss for how to assist. Vocational rehabilitation must accept criticism for ignoring the vocational needs of this population. The organization continues to provide services to other disability groups with more obvious impairments, yet uses the excuse that the LD population cannot be considered the "severest of the severe" despite the eventual impact on their personal and professional lives.

Budgetary concerns over the large numbers of people with LD that might overwhelm their services has unfortunately led the vocational rehabilitation personnel to turn their backs on one of the most underrepresented, unemployed, impoverished minorities in this country. As long as the Department of Vocational Rehabilitation continues to promote its 1960s vocational assessment process, it is doubtful that LD will be given the respect and entitlement to services that is shared by other disability groups.

Times are getting better for persons with LD, however. More are entering colleges and universities than ever before. Some experience success with technology and pursue their levels of advancement in their fields. Others experience success as entrepreneurs and appear in almost every aspect of working America. However, the numbers are still nonrepresentative of the total number of employed and parallel the statistics of the disabled unemployed.

In summary, the learning disabled have always been within the lining of mainstream America, living among the public. Some become successful, acquiring notoriety, and others are unable to compete with societal expectations. Schools still provide the most accurate projections on the number of people with learning disabilities that will become outcasts, misfits or troubled youth. Most will leave school and avoid calling attention to themselves and lead invisible lives, choosing to be elusive in the fabric of our communities, unless they surface trying to fight against the barriers of larger social systems.

11

The Mental Health Paradox: Helping or Harming

There is no quibbling about the fact that practicing child therapists and counselors working in the field of education use the DSMMD to explain the range of behaviors in school-age children whether a label is required or not. The hope is that, with a given diagnosis from the DSMMD, a gateway to treatment will open that will ameliorate if not eliminate behavioral and learning problems. The treatments of choice have narrowly focused on providing medications or psychotherapy. What begins to emerge out of this choice is a mental health paradox, a question of whether the use of medication or psychotherapy is actually helping or harming people in the quest to find the most appropriate treatment for a particular problem.

The problem arises when professionals internalize and apply DSMMD diagnoses without regard for the child's developmental level or school-related social context. The DSMMD can truly complicate, if not screw up, the next twenty years of young life with the labeling process. Not only is the label devastating in itself, but it often justifies the use of medications that may be used with perhaps devastating consequences for children and teens.

The *CBS Evening News* with Dan Rather dated April 15, 2004, described how the anti-depressant Serzone has been linked to suicidal behavior. Canada and Europe apparently have already banned the use of Serzone. This can only raise questions about why it is still being distributed in the US.

Earlier that same evening on ABC's national newscast, Peter Jennings presented a similar news piece on how anti-depressants have been connected with suicidal behavior in teens. The newscast also discussed the Food and Drug Administration's response to their involvement or lack thereof. In particular, the FDA had ignored, if not rejected, one study conducted about the relationship of anti-depressants to suicidal behavior in teens. Later, the FDA responded to the criticism by suggesting that it plans to conduct its own study.

One month earlier, in March of 2004, there was quite a stir on the national news about the use of several anti-depressants, including Paxil and Lexapro, and their connection to suicidal behavior in adults. The news did not stop there, however. ABC *Primetime* on December 15, 2004, aired a story which criticized the drug companies which hid from the public their own research findings which stated several dangerous side effects associated with the ingestion of Paxil.

On September 3, 2004, a story aired on *Good Morning America* about a young man about to go on trial for killing his grandparents when he was twelve years old. The young man made a statement to the effect that had he not been given Zoloft by professionals to treat the mental disorder clinical depression, he would not have killed his beloved grandparents. He went on to say that after taking the drug he felt unexplainable anger against the world. He heard voices telling him to get a gun and to follow through with the killing, something that he would never otherwise have done. Perhaps this young man did not need a label, nor a drug from a professional, to figure out what his real life problems were.

The FDA issued its own statement about a study conducted on the effects of Zoloft. The study results showed that there has been no propensity for violence found in individuals taking Zoloft as compared to those persons who were taking a placebo. How is the public to trust the FDA when so many questions can be raised about the side effects of many of the drugs one can access over the counter at the supermarket and even those drugs whose prescriptions are filled on a regular basis by the family doctor?

How far will drug companies go in advertising their products? In a country that seems obsessed with patrolling and policing illegal drugs, and imposing control over known medical drugs coming in from places like Canada, a contradiction lies in having the pharmaceutical companies (with the green light of the FDA) push expensive drugs without restriction of their usage. It goes as far as, for example, producing drugs such as Strattera for combating the negative symptoms of attention deficit disorder in adults. On December 5, 2004, CBS' *60 Minutes* aired a story about the use of Strattera. Strattera is one of the new drugs in a series of what has been called lifestyle drugs. The casualness of suggesting that those who may think that they suffer from attention deficit disorder can access this drug by asking the family doctor treats the whole disability phenomenon as if one can simply take a pill for a headache and life will improve. Attention deficit disorder is not new in adults and many Americans having ADD would dispute that somehow they acquired the invisible disability as if it were a virus to be caught like the common cold. It is misleading and downright irresponsible to be pushing lifestyle drugs as if one could expect that by popping chewing gum on a regular basis one would lose weight.

Regardless of how consumers think these issues are harmful or harmless, the responsible questions must be raised again. Why are drugs used with children and teens instead of psychotherapy? Why is it that this nation has turned to drugs to provide all the answers to human suffering, while waging a "War on Drugs" on another front? Is anyone really listening at all? If this is any indication of what trouble lies ahead, more than just a few questions will need to be asked about the role of the FDA, and pharmaceutical companies, as well as the employment of such drugs by mental health professionals.

Even as the drug debate goes on, however, it is harder than you might think to get public support to rally against the employment of drugs with children and teens. With children diagnosed with attention deficit hyperactivity disorder, Ritalin has long been the drug of choice. Parents swear by the positive results, claiming that their children with hyperactivity become well behaved and in control. However, the long term health risks of using such powerful drugs cannot be ignored. These children will grow up needing better ways to manage their lives than turning to drugs as the ultimate solution.

The Other Side of the Coin

The issue of drugs only intensifies because professionals cannot agree on what constitutes a disorder vs. a disability. While it may be appropriate in some cases to consider drugs as one alternative, the choice of psychotherapy for some children may be an inappropriate or unnecessary professional intervention.

Co-author Kristie Madsen had the experience of meeting a friend for lunch who worked in the area as a school social worker. After some time the friend commented: "The children I work with all have disabilities. Isn't it obvious that any child with ADD needs counseling? It should just be written into the child's Individualized Education Plan. These kids need it more than other children, don't they?"

The obvious stereotypic assumption echoed here is that if you are a disabled child you must obviously be mentally at risk. There is nothing implicit in having a disability that would mean that the child in question absolutely needs mental health counseling. In fact, the truth is that many teachers lack the training to work with a child having attention deficit disorder in their classrooms. Teachers may mean well, but they are often under pressure to complete their lesson plans and maintain conformity with no discipline problems at any cost. As a result, it is not uncommon for teachers to advocate secretly for a more restrictive school placement for certain hyperactive students because they don't want disruptions in their classes. Sensitivity training that focuses on shaping classroom accommodations to meet the needs of students having ADD is the core issue, not the need to medicate, readjust the child, or remove the child from the classroom.

One quakes hearing the news that authors are publishing new books that identify the bi-polar child. Even though there is an arena for research on the subject of childhood disorders, it seems that these persons who require the most protection in our society will be too quickly labeled, unjustly exposed and exploited long before there is enough legitimacy to carry such a devastating label throughout a lifetime.

As children grow into adults, the public can expect that the labels we have ascribed to them as children will be internalized. Professional attitudes and treatment plans likewise will contribute to that child's long range psychological development in ways that will not be conducive to mental health.

In fact, everyone can be assured that a whole new epidemic of problem behaviors that psychotherapists have in their treatment plans will be manifested in a variety of that child's social environments. In schools, there will be an explosion of individualized education plans and more classroom segregation of children from their peers.

If professionals are unwilling to question what role ethics plays in the use of the DSMMD, it is doubtful that they will be doing anything more than feeding the problem at hand. Or at least, in effect, creating a monster where once there was a child.

There is nothing so egregious as a professional who can not identify normal social and emotional developmental milestones. In one example, co-author Kristie Madsen observed how one school psychologist who was not familiar with the normal age appropriate social and emotional development interpreted one child's behavior so that it fit into the guidelines for emotional disturbance, even when it was clear that the child was exhibiting age appropriate behaviors. Because the child was showing noncompliant behaviors, the child was removed from the regular classroom on the basis of having oppositional defiant disorder even though the child had previously been diagnosed as learning disabled. In this instance it was difficult to tell whether this professional grasped or cared about the differences.

In another instance, a local child psychologist described a case that he was concerned about to Kristie. He described a ten year old child's fantasy about being desirable to the opposite sex as the child being delusional. Kristie had a basic understanding of the child's developmental level. As they discussed the psychologist's assessment of the child's behaviors, Kristie began to wonder if this could really be the same child. Kristie considered what she knew; the end result of needing, but never receiving, enough love looked much the same as any child who might invent an imagined playmate. Beyond the obvious problem with the above scenario, the child psychologist is an example of someone who carries this view of pathology into every situation, shining such attitudes on children that need the most help.

12

Special Forever: A Kid's Worst Nightmare!

Self-contained special education classrooms that focus on children with emotional disturbance (ED) or learning disability (LD) are not always the best avenues for children who don't fit the mainstream of the school system. There are children who enter into this kind of segregated classroom for any number of reasons.

For example, children with reading disabilities who have acted out their anger because they have been ostracized by peers and teachers following their failures have been placed in such a program. Because of their disruptions in class they were removed to the more restrictive classroom after having been newly diagnosed with conduct disorder, oppositional defiant disorder, implosive disorder, or with the special education designator, emotionally disturbed (ED).

Special education classes have served as detainment spots for the children where they are expected to learn what is socially appropriate in isolation from the social environment that most impacted them. It seems rather odd that the school personnel would expect that learning social rules would magically occur outside the context of being with peers.

The segregation does not induce social conformity in most instances but makes for a temporary band-aid on the real problem. It is also difficult to understand how the child can learn new behaviors to supplant old ones if the original problem lies elsewhere.

Any one of us would throw a tantrum if punished over and over because of the inability to turn handsprings. The same is true for children who lack the capacity to read, write, do math or attend.

Strangely the relationship between a poor family situation and school failure or the inability to deal with learning disability issues escapes the attention of professional counselors. All children would show anger if they live with alcoholic behavior all the time, or are beaten for not performing correctly in school. Perhaps being traumatized by violence in the family or neighborhood might mean for many children that they can't concentrate on studies. It has become easier to label using the DSMMD and segregate than to disrupt the ordinary flow of the classroom.

The most important and debilitating aspect of removing the child to a more restrictive arrangement, however, is the unethical practice of making new diagnoses of emotional disturbance whereby children remain labeled with a mental disorder for the rest of their school years. The devastating consequences are:

1. the diagnosed learning disability and emotional difficulties related to it are not addressed;
2. the child remains in an inappropriate school placement, segregated from peers;
3. the label of emotional disturbance remains fixed in the child's records which impacts how the child will be served by school officials, and other important persons in the child's life; will affect the way the child internalizes the label and feels about himself;
4. the individual will forever have diminished opportunities as a result of being labeled emotionally disturbed.

13

Everyone Needs a Label, Don't They?

The confusion over a DSMMD diagnosis can really get messy in a different arena: that of adults with disabilities. Because they are less malleable than their younger counterparts, adults do not always succumb so easily to mental health intervention.

Within the college setting where Kristie Madsen worked for nine years, students were referred to community professionals for testing to either identify a disability or to re-confirm a disability status. After students returned, they voiced their complaints to Kristie about the diagnostic process.

Students described how disillusioned they were by the attitudes of diagnosticians toward them and their desires for school accommodations. Other concerns expressed were about how family, peers and instructors would react to the current information about their disability since they were not sure exactly how much or what not to say about the intimate details. Most frequently the question could be heard: "What guarantee will I have that this diagnosis won't screw with my life now and in the future?"

Yet, other concerns students voiced had to do with the final report on their disability and the lack of professional guidance students felt they received from the professional once the testing was over. One student expressed it this way: "This professional got all this money to say what he wanted about me and my life, but I am the one still left wondering about what it all means."

Another student commented about how the professional reacted to her while she was finding out that she had ADD or attention deficit disorder. "I expected to feel differently about myself, but suddenly I was being treated by the professional as if I was some leper."

Students complained that they were given diagnoses without having received enough information about what the disability actually was. They were not provided with adequate information that would in their minds justify the kind of diagnosis they received, especially with regards to the additional parts of the evaluation referring to mental or emotional status.

Common complaints surfaced about diagnosticians and their lack of sensitivity to the student's real, adverse life situations. Students stated that the professionals seemed over pre-occupied with the test results, as if the person did not matter.

For students diagnosed with clinical depression, anxiety disorder, or bi-polar, the most common question seemed to center on "what validity does this diagnosis have in my life?" Students diagnosed with mental illness were left to wonder what the whole purpose behind testing was and if having this label for the purposes of accommodations would bring anything positive into their lives.

One student expressed it this way: "It certainly doesn't make me feel better about myself. Although I have always known that I was anxious, how will this help me to take tests any better in the classroom?"

When some students approached their diagnosticians with questions about the diagnosis, the professionals seemed lacking in how to guide them. After having read the diagnostician's reports, students were often left in the dark with understanding the test results and were not given the chance to interact with the diagnostician about their impressions.

It should be recognized that not all diagnosticians were regarded harshly by students. In fact, quite a few were appreciated for their skill, knowledge, sensitivity and communication with students.

For the students who were disgruntled, however, they reported that more emotional damage was done as a result of having gone through the testing experience. They reported how disenfranchised they felt by having been labeled or passed off as just depressed.

One college student summed up beautifully the whole experience and her feelings about having been diagnosed with attention deficit disorder and clinical depression.

"The minute I set foot in his office, I knew instantly what he was going to do and say because every therapist has treated me the same way. I have been to four, trying to find someone who can see my life the way I do. The last one wanted to talk about my childhood experiences with my father and mother instead of what was happening to my life now. He was so busy trying to 'treat' my 'depressed mindset' instead of listening to me.

He didn't hear me when I said I failed the test in school because the teacher didn't believe that I needed test accommodations. He didn't hear how much I hurt when the teacher rejected my request for extended time in his office. I wanted help with how to get along in a university setting with my disability, not get into a heavy discussion over my past. No offense but Prozac can't help me talk any better to my teacher. I want to accept my disability as part of myself but its hard when a therapist tells you that you are simply depressed, have test anxiety and you lack self-confidence and not that there is any sort of disability issue going on. I felt really invalidated by the experience and I don't need one more label to describe what's wrong with me. He really doesn't get my disability at all. It's me that has to live with other people that don't understand how my life changes because of it [the disability]."

14

Looking Beyond the Label to Serve Every Client

The last few chapters have focused primarily on how the DSMMD does not serve every client. Is there another approach that psychotherapists can use, if the DSMMD is not the driving force behind psychotherapy? Co-author Peter Leech has spent thirty years of his clinical practice developing an approach that focuses on the functioning and life challenges of his clients. The next few chapters will describe an approach based on what the clients bring with them to the therapy sessions. Aspects of this approach will address how to assess a client's functioning and appropriate direction for therapy goals.

Times have changed in the field of psychotherapy over the years. The focus has become centered on defining the person with a diagnostic label. Therapists are having to pull a label out of the DSMMD that matches the client's symptoms, and having that label be the problem with the client rather than address some of the real problems. This is particularly true with regards to clients who are moving from one agency to another, or one system of care to another, none of which are satisfying to the needs that the client has. In finding the meaning of the actual problem, the one that the client defines as the problem, the therapist can begin to work in such a way that is validating to the client.

Getting beyond the label is where the therapist needs to begin. It is empowering to the client to be heard identifying what is causing the hurt. For the therapist to acknowledge the hurt in some clear way tends to validate the client's sense of self, that the client is intact to some degree.

The therapist can then begin to work with the client around that sense of intactness of self that is the keystone toward moving the client back to the healthy self, or higher level of functioning. With this stronger sense of intactness, the client will have the ability to withstand some of the hardships of interacting in larger social systems that must be addressed.

No matter what the losses are, or disability experienced, that sense of self must be re-discovered and re-claimed by the client. The therapist is in the position of validating that self, helping the client to operate from a position of strength.

When a therapist is asking for advice on what to do with a person who is depressed or, how to deal with a person who has lost a loved one, or someone who has lost a limb, the answer is the same. Underneath the person who is depressed or mourning or disabled there is the self of the person that has not changed. Getting in touch with that person's self concept is more important than working with the client toward accepting the loss, or being disabled. Working with the intact self, then, is the goal of the therapist. Moving beyond the label to re-enforce what is healthy or intact in the client's sense of self is far more important than re-enforcing the notion that the person is somehow a different person because of the experience.

Often it is the maltreatment by other people that forces the client to lose his sense of self and adopt a new, more negative self image in accordance with societal expectations. Often it is the range of losses that the client has experienced that re-enforces the notion that the self is lost as well.

Getting at the Heart of What Matters to Clients

Getting at the heart of what matters to clients is a function of not focusing exclusively on the label that a client brings to therapy. When clients say that they have been referred because they are said by another person to be depressed or experiencing panic attacks, the approach should be that, while being depressed, or panicked is problematic for the client, it is not the problem.

While these experiences are very uncomfortable and disturbing to the client, they simply are not the problem. The actual problem is something that lies beneath the surface of the symptoms.

One of the strategies that has been used over the years to discern what is really the problem is to ask the client "when" it was that the feelings of depression or panic attacks began. As clients begin to think about when it all started, a follow up question can be asked which focuses on what was going on in their lives at the time when it all started.

When the therapist begins to get from the client a description of events during the recent past, the entire context of the problem begins to emerge. A three-dimensional matrix of how the client lives or has lived is revealed as each aspect of life surfaces.

For example the client might describe where he lived and with whom. He is able to focus on what he was doing at the time, for example, going to school or working, or not doing these things. As the client continues to describe events, he can be asked to examine the exact nature of the relationship he had to the job, or to discuss the nature of the relationships he had to the people.

Through this type of exploration into the person's place in time, the therapist can begin to see the primary forces that have shaped the feelings of discomfort the client may call depression, or panic.

The vast majority of people who seek out services from social agencies or mental health clinicians are people who have encountered some loss in their lives. The loss may be one of those more widely recognized, such as the death of a loved one (spouse, child, parent), or physical loss (paralysis or amputation).

The loss may be one less widely recognized, such as loss of relationship through separation or divorce, loss of a job due to loss of market, downsizing, or retirement. It may be even more subtle than any of the above, but no less profound for the individual, such as the existence of a learning disability, loss of physical stamina, visual acuity or memory related to aging, the physical losses related to chronic illness or mild brain injury.

Whatever these losses, the individuals who experience them will have emotional responses to them that are predictable only in that they will occur. The specific nature of them cannot be anticipated. Moreover, each primary loss will have secondary effects that will accrue as time goes by. These secondary effects can be called the secondary losses to the individual.[1]

Each of these, in turn, will have emotional responses attached to them. In a like manner to the primary loss, the specific nature of the responses cannot be anticipated. These responses—for example, sadness, anger, fear, guilt—are quite natural human responses, congruous to the situation, and are not necessarily pathological.

As the therapist begins to perceive the primary and secondary forces that have occurred in the client's life and discern the emotional responses that have accrued to each, the real nature of what is troubling to the client begins to be revealed.

Take, for example, a client who has lost a job. The reason for losing the job will determine some of the client's emotional response to the situation. Was the client fired for some reason? Did the management downsize? Did the big boss suddenly die from a heart attack? Losing a job is a big deal, but the emotional reaction one might have to the primary event will vary.

Consider next the secondary effects, for example, the economic challenges related to having lost a job, and any fears about that. How the person feels about himself or herself as a person without a job, for example, with whom do they identify, whether or not they esteem themselves as productive, contributing members of the family, community, or society.

Another example of a common event for most people is retirement from a job. An individual who may have been seen as a person who has achieved fame and fortune may suddenly find himself in retirement as a person who has nothing to do in the world. This may be a serious loss for this person.

The loss associated with having retired has secondary effects. For example, secondary effects may include one's general self esteem, one's ability to know what to do with oneself in the world, one's ability to continue to have the kind of relationships that were common in the working world. Any number of aspects of a person's life can begin to be discerned if a therapist looks beyond the label or presenting symptoms.

The problem with the DSMMD and its heavy use and focus for treatment is that the therapist's energy gets stuck on the label. Instead of really focusing on starting where the client is and allowing the client to define the problem, the client is viewed as simply depressed.

Within the DSMMD's Five Axis Diagnosis, there is a place to refer to some of the environmental and social factors that impact clients, but not really in a way that classifies factors in order of importance or severity.

One example that comes to mind are those clients who may have trouble sustaining themselves because of health problems that interfere with their continuing to work. They may not be seen as disabled enough to qualify for a disability check or SSI. They may need to ask a social welfare agency for general assistance money in order to survive.

The act of asking for financial assistance can be degrading to the individual in and of itself. The forces involved with defining one's self as a person who needs that support or help, coupled with the negative attitudes of those people who are supposed to be service providers, can combine to produce an even greater trauma than the simple fact that the individual is without a job or money. It is the interaction with the larger social system that is traumatic to him and may become an additional secondary loss for the individual (see Chapter 21).

Clients have reported that they have felt worthless after such interactions with service providers. They perceive that the service provider sees them as a person who is a potential cheater in the system or non-deserving of financial support.

Others have shared their experiences about the negative attitudes they received when they take their food stamps into the supermarket. They need to use the stamps to buy essential food items, yet they are looked at by cashiers as less than worthy or eyed with suspicion. The treatment is brief and curt from cashiers but in that instant, they are made to feel worse that they don't have their own money to take into the store to buy the things that they need. It is the interactions with people whom the client perceives as judgmental, as well as having to reveal one's financial difficulties publicly, that becomes the additional trauma to the client.

15

The Acknowledgment Approach

In *Acknowledgement*,[1] co-author Peter Leech defined his "acknowledgment approach" as addressing "what is—" about a person's concern and life. When discussing the situation of people with health problems or disabilities or any loss of function, it is important to address the reality of that loss with the clients.

Questions that are important to address include:

- In what way does the loss of function affect their lives?
- In what ways have their daily lives changed because of it?
- In what ways have their relationships changed because of it?
- How have their previous states of functioning changed?
- How have their images of themselves changed?
- How have their perceptions of themselves changed in relation to everything else in the world?

These issues need to be taken up on a very individual basis with each client. Often the very nature of the relationship to the broader world, or connection to society, has changed as well.

For example, being able to participate at a level of equality or equity has often changed for persons with acquired disabilities. These people are aware that others may view them as lesser than, if it is clear that they can't function at the same level as that society construes for the average person.

Societal attitudes do affect how individuals with disabilities see themselves. Individuals are aware intuitively that when they are viewed as having less function, there may be the interpretation that they are purposefully malingering or not wanting to participate.

Other negative attitudes are clearly evident when fully functioning people discourage the participation of persons who cannot fully function up to social expectations. The idea behind the stigma of disability is that the persons are identified by the dysfunctional qualities, not as the dimensional whole persons that they are.

There are emotions attached to being treated differently because of a disability, or experiencing negative attitudes from other people.

There are emotions attached to having lost something in your life that you cared about. If there has been a loss of body function, feelings of sadness often follow. And that sadness can be a profound experience as the person begins to understand all the losses that go hand in hand with the changes that have happened.

Too often in our culture, people are told not to pay attention to these emotions. The old adage is, "if you will just accept this thing, everything will be ok."

Most people are smarter than that. They can see the lie in it. The acknowledgement approach simply opens the issue up so the person can look at the loss and see it for what it is and react to it with feeling.

In other words, if you are feeling sad, you are feeling sad. It relates to something you lost and how much you cared about it. You are likely to feel sad about the investment you had in the ability you once had. The magnitude of the sadness will relate to the magnitude of the loss.

The same can be said about feeling anger. The magnitude of the anger will be the same magnitude as the loss they experience. The kind of hurts that accompany loss often take the form of economic deprivation, changes in the ability to participate, attitudinal changes of being seen as lesser than, being treated as if one never functioned better than one functions now. Those kinds of hurts create a great deal of anger.

If the feelings the person has are not acknowledged, the person puts energy into trying to avoid the experience of sadness or anger. All of the energy it takes to keep the magnitude of the feeling down, which is related to the loss, won't be available for the person to do other activities. It is that level of loss of energy that may be viewed as the depressive feature.

It is commonly expected that clients who have sustained serious loss in their lives will become depressed. One reason that these clients become depressed is that they learn denial at the hands of experts.

That is to say, these clients stop talking about what is actually going on with them to the degree that they put all their energy into trying not to see things as they really are or to make them appear better than they are.

The acknowledgement approach simply says, open it up, see things as they are. Reclaim your energy by at least acknowledging you have some anger. Also acknowledge that there are some things that are unacceptable losses.

Therapists who understand the concept of loss and their role of acknowledging their client's losses are not apt to experience what is commonly referred to (in the language of psychotherapy) as client resistance. Client resistance may be the result of a failure on the part of the therapist to define the problem as the client sees it.

16

Assessment Approaches

As any social worker will tell you, an ecosystems perspective is the most comprehensive approach to evaluating the "person within the environment."[1] The DSMMD, however, is indisputably the most widely used reference tool.

There is an alternative to the DSMMD that may be appreciated for its more comprehensive approach to clients who have health conditions, disabilities and functional limitations. The International Classification of Function, Disability and Health (ICF) that was developed by the World Health Organization[2] offers a more dimensional view of clients than the DSMMD and Five Axis diagnostic model. There is no reliance on a specific diagnostic label that defines the treatment approach, nor the negative consequences that can occur from misapplication of diagnostic labels. The ICF offers a much better representation of the range of issues that the average client experiences.

One of the important aspects of the ICF in the psychotherapeutic process is its emphasis on client function, not pathology. It views the individual as part of an entire social context and considers the interactive nature of human behavior in the environment.

While discussing bodily function, and conditions under which individuals perform on a daily basis, it is positive in its approach to identifying other outside factors that may impact the way the individual behaves in the particular circumstances. It highlights the role of social context, such as a person in job context, and establishes the nature of the relationship between the two.

The ICF addresses body structures and functions as well as outside environmental factors that could shape the way the client thinks or reacts. It helps the therapist to assess personal life challenges in a way that the DSMMD cannot.

The ICF in its grouping of factors recognizes, acknowledges, and classifies the impact of such environmental factors. It is more accurate and easier to focus on the client's actual problem, rather than relying on a label alone to determine how to proceed with the client.

The environmental factors include a wide range of issues central to many clients. To take one example, societal attitudes within agencies is discussed. Too often in recent years, agencies that were originally designed to serve the client have begun to function as barriers because of the creation of impenetrable policies and criteria for eligibility. The ICF describes the connection of service to client. It defines what the expectation should be: that there should be a useful service that comes out of service-client connection. It categorizes whether the situation a client faces is an existing barrier or a facilitator in the client's life.

The idea behind the category is to see whether an existing agency provides a service which is accessible, non-existent or withheld from the client because of some arbitrary requirement that the system has employed to maintain itself. This makes it easier for the therapist to understand the client when the client expresses frustration at not receiving the service, experiencing attitude discrimination, or describing barriers to accessing the system.

For example, there was a client who applied to General Assistance because he was injured on the job and sustained a serious back injury. The client was told that the injury could not be resolved by having surgery. In fact, according to the client's doctor, surgery would be too dangerous, more dangerous than the actual injury. The client also was told by the doctor that the medical system would not become involved with any surgery unless he was in such intolerable pain that there were no other options. His only recourse was to live with the pain. The doctor also told him that he should not continue to do the sort of work he did before. The client was dismayed that he would be unable to return to the work he had done before. He was even more devastated when he applied and was rejected for Social Security Disability on the grounds that he looked to any outside observer as if he should be able to work.

Eventually, this client found himself in the position of running out of state disability money and applying for General Assistance. He needed the money to survive.

As he approached the office of General Assistance, he noticed the glances and hardened stares of the staff workers from behind the counter. He wondered if they thought he was trying to cheat the system because, after all, he looked as if he should be able to work. He realized after he went home that their questions and negative attitudes in dealing with him at the counter seemed to imply that they had thought he was just trying to go around and collect money from the system. They were communicating suspicion that they did not believe that he had a physical disability, treating him as if he were reluctant to go back to work. They asked that he go back and talk to a former employer first about returning to work.

The client did approach his former employer about returning to work. The employer said to the client, "Not on my life can I employ you again. My insurance rates would go out of sight with someone having your medical history."

Not knowing what else to do, he returned to Social Services feeling that he had no hope of being served in a positive way and told the service workers what his employer had said. They appeared indifferent to his situation and told him to keep trying to get work.

The client conveyed to them how angry he was about his financial situation and their reactions. The social service workers referred to him as emotionally unstable because he showed them feelings of anger.

This illustrates how hostile a system can be and feel to a person who is trying to make the transition from a normal work life to a new life as a disabled non-worker, trying to access financial resources in the community.

The ICF enables therapists to look at individual functioning, to pinpoint exactly what the limitation is and how the limitations impact how the individual is able to interact within immediate social surroundings. Also it can help the client to focus on how the effect of the social response impacts the emotional state.

The ICF, along with the acknowledgement approach, can be used to ascertain which bed of losses and functional limitations the individual is dealing with and, if possible, to determine what actual environmental barriers exist for the client.

No matter what methods may be used by the therapist, obtaining an accurate assessment of what is really going on in the client's life is essential. To find a therapeutic direction there is a need to assess the client's abilities, strengths and limitations in functioning with accuracy.

While the ICF is an important tool in determining a range of possible factors, it is still one of many tools that should be used with clients. The DSMMD alone will not yield the most dimensional approach to working with any client.

17

The Role of the Therapist

Most clients are perceptive enough to know if their reality is being addressed by the therapist. If a therapist suggests a client is just depressed, there will be little investment on the part of the client to do the work necessary to move out of the depressed place. The therapist has the responsibility to understand what is really happening in the client's life and begin to open up the specific issues in order to see what needs to be addressed. This will free the client's energies to focus on the work ahead.

The role of the therapist is often discussed at professional groups. Many new roles have emerged than there were years ago for the private practicing therapist. Coaching clients has become a new and growing aspect of work. Becoming an advocate with or for clients seems more controversial to some therapists.

One thing that cannot change as part of the therapist's role is that of being a role model for the client, modeling a healthy relationship with the client. It can be perhaps the first equitable relationship the person has had.

The importance of forming an alliance with the client cannot be underestimated. It has to be a part of the relationship because of the trust factor that must be maintained in order for therapeutic goals to be achieved. It is difficult to move a distrustful client toward any pre-set goals or agendas the therapist has. It is even more difficult to convince resistant clients that they need to be motivated to do the work because they need to accept the therapist's perspective of their problems. As mentioned above, a resistant client is one whose fears have not been addressed and the therapist may be out of touch with what the client cares about. Where resistance seems insurmountable, therapists need to reexamine whether their own issues may be interfering with their ability to be effective. When the trust in the therapeutic alliance has been broken, or is irreparable, the therapist has the responsibility to refer the client on to another therapist. Getting at the heart of what matters to the client should be the goal of every therapist, and validation of every client.

Myth III

The Mental Health System Is Accessible to the Disadvantaged

Introduction: No Clear Pathways to the Mental Health System

Clients, whether having mental illness or not, share complicated lives that sometimes seem too impossible for therapists to help at any level. Their lives seem to be lost in the folds of larger social systems that have become rigid barriers to the receipt of basic services.

Because most agencies rely on one another to self perpetuate and are so deeply entrenched in their own policies, they do not recognize how interdependent and confusing they have become for the average consumer. Nor do they understand that the consequences of their practices result in treating clients unfairly. It is more than rejection of the services however. There is also a climate of inhospitality that comes with approaching social systems for help. Along with the rigidity of agency standards, consumers complain that there is also a climate of emotional abusiveness that goes on and is expressed by vendors of these social services. Consumers are made to feel minimized when they ask for help. The attitude seems to stem back in history to English Poor Law[1] in which there was a need to believe that for persons to receive financial support, they must prove they are deserving of our caring; that is by "pulling themselves up by their own boot straps."

Struggling to elevate their lives, persons on the lower end of the socio-economic totem pole find themselves caught up in a type of oppressive agency sub-culture, one where consumers are treated with suspicion, having to prove their worthiness as the poorest of the poor and endure experiences that are humiliating because they are the most financially exploitable people in our society. Individuals who are victimized through their encounters with a network of social service agencies are in effect, experiencing system induced trauma.

It is doubtful that anyone has taken the time to ask if such agencies are truly accessible to those in our communities who are most needy. Or to ask if the services provided are valuable once the policies that were meant to bridge service gaps become barriers in themselves.

The labeling process has expanded to encompass how social services are distributed nationwide. Labeling consumers within the social system network has become a new language through which social system agencies communicate to each other in order to provide services to consumers. Unfortunately there are devastating consequences to consumers for using labeling as part of the criteria for the inclusion or exclusion of social services. Consumers experience system induced trauma, emotional trauma resulting from being cast out of a variety of services because one does not fit neatly into the labeling system.

In many scenarios which will be presented in the next few chapters, clients become stuck in agency quicksand, trying to obtain a service that will sustain some aspect of their existence, to fit into the right criteria based on: family, evidence of dependents, monetary assets, health insurance, ability to work, need for food stamps or General Assistance, need for government subsidized housing, eligibility for Social Security Income or eligibility for state disability funds, vocational training, public or private mental health, drug rehabilitation and medical programs.

The psychotherapist who has clients who are trying to access social services in order to survive is often at a loss how to be helpful. Most professional clinical training does not involve working with clients around the issues of system barriers. Dealing with clients and social systems cannot be ignored, however. If clients suffer because they are so pre-occupied with how they will survive, how they will fit into a social system, they are emotionally unavailable to focus on their own emotional needs which is counterproductive to therapy.

The following cases are true to the extent that the major events did occur in the lives of these clients. The names and details have been deliberately changed, however, to protect the true identities of clients.

The authors have provided an analysis of ways that the clinician can build bridges in the community and close gaps in services while still working productively with clients one on one.

18

Case: Joey

Joey felt generally ill and nauseous most of the time. He had been diagnosed with Hepatitis C, asthma, low vision and seizures of unknown etiology, occurring only when Joey was feeling stressed. He admitted that he had been a "street drunk" most of his life, having dropped out of school when he was in the ninth grade because he "just couldn't keep up with learning."

He had supported himself with occasional employment and odd jobs until he had become too ill to work and was diagnosed two years previously with Hepatitis C. After diagnosis he stopped drinking altogether. He no longer had the urge to drink because he felt nauseous all the time. Because he could not work, Joey applied for Supplemental Security Income (SSI) but had been denied several times. Hepatitis C was not considered a valid reason for not returning to work.

The only safety net for Joey, therefore, was General Assistance and food stamps provided through the Department of Social Services. When social services processed his application and learned of his history of alcoholism, they were concerned about whether any money they would be giving him would be used to support "his habit," and devised a program with which he needed to comply in order to receive the assistance.

The program required Joey to come to town each week so that they could follow his progress, made mental health counseling mandatory, and required him to check in with the local substance abuse treatment program, and attend local AA meetings. The general assistance check was sent directly to his landlord to cover three hundred dollars for rent.

The food stamps helped cover his contribution in his shared housing arrangement with other men who also had limited financial situations. There was no money for him to use for transportation costs.

The location of the house he resided in was eight miles out of town, so Joey could try to attend weekly meetings in town only when he was able to hitchhike or catch occasional rides from his landlord. Beyond a few vouchers Social Services would not provide for transportation costs to support Joey's attempts to comply with their expectations, and remained unchanged in their position: that Joey needed to maintain attendance at the meetings and had to find his own transportation at his own cost or risk losing General Assistance funds.

In meetings with his therapist, Joey described that he was too exhausted and sick to be able to walk to all his appointments in town. He expressed anger over the fact that there was no acknowledgement from Social Services that he had not touched a drink in over two years, and the restrictions were unnecessary.

Joey's physical state began to deteriorate. He found it difficult to eat because of his nausea. He became extremely thin and underweight. He could not sleep. His asthma was a continual problem because of his rural living surroundings. If he became too emotionally stressed, he experienced seizures (that no one had yet diagnosed.)

Joey attempted suicide, taking most of his pills in one night. He was treated in the emergency room, and released, the suicide attempt being seen as not very serious because he was considered a drunk. In meetings with his therapist, Joey spoke frankly about his limited interest in continuing to live because he felt so sick all the time, frightened about his physical problems and barely able to comply with the social service plan.

Joey continued to meet with his therapist when he could but he was losing hope of ever returning to a normal life, one that did not require being on a treadmill going from one appointment to another and from one agency to another while not getting any real help with his physical problems. His therapist could only assess Joey's primary problem as being so pressured emotionally to attend all the meetings in order to survive that he was becoming despondent and run down. Joey became so physically ill that he no longer felt a desire to live. How could Joey be helped?

Consultation and Approach to Client

In the above scenario, labels are used by human service entities for the purposes of identifying, defining, clarifying and simplifying both the procedural guidelines and eligibility standards of the organization. The use of diagnostic labeling to classify individuals applying for services has become deeply entrenched in the distribution of social services. Individuals like Joey are often caught between systems trying to comply with the expectations of each organization, and yet do not receive the services they need in order to survive.

In this instance, Joey was labeled as a person who was alcoholic because of his past history of alcohol abuse. The label followed Joey by way of his confidential records and traveled through a variety of human hands and service offices unquestioned, as if the label still applied to him in his present state. Consequently, Joey was treated as if he was the very essence of the label he was given. A myriad of agency requirements followed which only compounded Joey's life challenges.

Joey's real need for a more comprehensive evaluation and medical follow up of his condition was overlooked. Instead he was introduced to additional institutional stresses that only worsened his situation.

As Joey began to feel the toll of dealing with system barriers and trying to comply with the eligibility requirements of social services, he began to lose hope. His feelings of helplessness and depression led to despair. In short, Joey was experiencing system induced trauma. The end result was that Joey's health declined. What could the therapist do in Joey's situation?

Clinical Interventions

1. Intervention with Social Services in order to reduce the unnecessary stresses in Joey's life.
2. Assistance with finding effective medical evaluation and treatment for Joey's multiple problems.
3. Provide new information from (2) to support Joey's application for SSI.

Therapeutic Value

1. Acknowledging the reality of the life situation that Joey presents validates Joey's sense of himself and contributes to the development of a stronger therapeutic alliance.
2. Joey can begin to concentrate on addressing his real life and health challenges and conserve mental energy that can be focused on therapy.
3. Joey can begin to believe that he can survive in the context of so many social service agencies, and confront system barriers from a position of strength and self-advocacy.

19

Case: Sally

Sally, a fifty-three-year-old white woman, was referred for therapy. She was the mother of two grown young men and had managed through her life fairly well. Throughout her life Sally had worked at several jobs, including nutritionist and certified nurse assistant. More recently she had taken a position in a private caregiver organization.

Sally described herself as a person who had struggled with a weight problem most of her life. One day while she was working, she felt out of sorts in a way she had never felt before. Because she had no health insurance at the time, Sally felt she could not go to the hospital and find out if she had a health problem. Continuing with her work was the last thing that Sally remembered as she collapsed on the job. When she awoke a number of days later in the hospital, she realized that she had been in intensive care.

The nurse arrived and to her surprise Sally was told that she was diabetic and had been in a deep coma. The nurse also told Sally that there was residual damage in which the toxins that were present during the coma had caused a serious neuropathy (lack of sensation) to occur.

The result was a numbness that Sally experienced from her feet up to her mid-torso. This phenomenon remained after she left the hospital and tried to function in her life again.

Over some months, Sally realized that the neuropathy was not resolving, that there were balance problems that accompanied her condition. After ten to fifteen minutes on her feet standing or moving around, Sally felt faint.

Everything became a major effort for Sally. She began to feel depressed because she felt incapable of managing her life. The feelings of loss about her own functionality deepened. The doctors told Sally that their pre-scribed anti-depressant medications had been the cause of her fainting spells.

They were sympathetic but encouraged her to continue taking the pills, and then referred her to a therapist to provide therapy for her depres-sion and to consider psychological testing to add to her application for Sup-plemental Security Income (SSI.) When Sally met with the therapist she was anxious and felt distraught about what was happening to her in her life. She had been thinking about SSI and was already receiving state dis-ability money which continued for a short while. She was hoping that her physical condition would resolve in time and she would be able to return to work.

This did not happen. Instead of resolving, her condition worsened. Her balance problems became more serious. Other symptoms appeared such as bowel incontinence. Her ability to participate in activities longer than fifteen minutes without becoming exhausted or faint impinged on her personal life as well.

Wishing to return to work, Sally approached her supervisor to explain what was happening to her. Her supervisor listened but was unwilling to re-employ Sally unless she recovered entirely.

It was then that Sally realized she had to do something different. She finally applied to SSI. Her application to SSI was denied the first time. She reapplied and the second time she was sent to be examined by a physician to determine the severity and functional limitations of her new disability. The physician did a thorough job and assured Sally that her limitations would certainly render her eligible for SSI. Sally later received notice that she had been denied assistance a second time.

Along with the letter of denial, suggestions were made that she return to her previous career track of a nutritionist. SSI was of the opinion that she could pursue working in the medical profession if she chose to with her bachelor of science degree. Sally was outraged. Not only was there no such job in her geographic area, but having a degree did not mean that she could be hired in the medical profession without additional school-ing. Her bachelor's degree had been obtained years before. She was now at a different juncture in her life. Furthermore, Sally was enraged because she could not even stand up without holding onto things to avoid falling down. To become a trained nutritionist it would take more than physical well-being, it required income, time and stamina.

Sally stared incredulously at the letter for a long time. She simply did not have any of those things in her present life. The whole picture did not match the world she was now living in. No one, it seemed, understood the daily uphill battle she was having with her body. As she read on in the letter she noticed where SSI had suggested that she had refused to see a neurologist. Nothing could be further from the truth than that.

Sally arranged an appointment to visit with a local neurologist, but, by the time the evaluation appointment was scheduled to occur, the second denial from SSI had come. The evaluation results were just being finished and thus were not available to SSI to support her case.

Despondent over SSI's denial a second time, Sally became deeply depressed. She felt inadequate because she was not anywhere near her previous level of functioning. Yet she was told to return to work.

Sally could not see a future for herself and attempted suicide by injecting herself with the insulin which she had been given to treat her diabetes. She had not anticipated that the long lasting insulin would not kill her. After she awoke the next day, the social worker who was assigned to assist her with the round of SSI application stopped for a visit. The social worker noticed that Sally had not started on the application and questioned why Sally was just getting out of bed at 4:00 in the afternoon. Sally, still shaken by the fact that she was alive, admitted to the social worker what she had done, that she had wanted to take her own life but had failed. Being a mandated reporter, the social worker felt it was her responsibility to report the matter to the authorities.

Sally was escorted by the police to the hospital. A counselor from mental health arrived to assess her state of mind. All Sally wanted to do now was to go home. Sally was assured by the mental health counselor that if she signed a contract to the effect that she would not commit suicide, she could leave the hospital. Sally signed it feeling humiliated and resigned.

On her way out, Sally asked if the counselor would convey information about the incident to her private therapist. The counselor agreed to do this. Upon returning home from the hospital, Sally decided that she needed a change. She left for six weeks to visit the members of her family who resided in Nevada.

Sally's therapist waited to set up a new appointment with her. During the time Sally was away, the mental health counselor never contacted Sally's therapist about her suicide attempt. Sally's therapist learned of the event when the sessions convened weeks later. After Sally visited the therapist's office, he called mental health to speak with the counselor who had been with Sally the day she tried to commit suicide. The counselor responded placidly to the therapist's questions, remarking cooly that Sally did not seem to be at risk to herself that morning in the hospital. Thus, the counselor had felt no burning need to contact Sally's private therapist or anyone else after Sally left the hospital.

When Sally returned to her home from her time away, feelings of isolation and depression returned. Once again Sally was faced with how she was going to transition into a new way of life as a disabled woman with no income base.

The social worker returned to her home to assist with the application for SSI once again and explained to Sally that she had a much better chance of receiving SSI now that she had attempted suicide. This dismayed Sally. She became very angry and frustrated by the fact that not only did she have to go through all the physical ramifications of a new disability that might make her eligible for SSI, but that she also had to be classified as mentally ill before she could receive SSI.

To date, Sally is waiting to hear if she will receive SSI. She tries to make ends meet on General Assistance and food stamps. How could the therapist help Sally?

Consultation and Approach to Client

Sally's case, like Joey's, speaks to the larger social questions that surround the use of labeling in the human service industries of today. The use of labeling has become so institutionalized into the operations of the health care system that average Americans are unaware of the impact it has had on their way of life.

Because labeling has become big business for health care providers and is now part of the "business as usual" attitude in the social service network, it has also become a way of controlling the very poorest, the most dependent consumers of social services like Sally. The most vulnerable and disenfranchised persons have now become the most exploitable because they are powerless to change a system in which the diagnostic label has gained so much power.

Sally's case also calls attention to the fact that reliance on diagnostic labels interferes with the actual process of distributing social services to those persons who need them the most. Persons like Sally, who don't fit neatly into the existing labeling categories of systems such as SSI, are denied access to these services because the label distinguishes those who receive services from those who do not, instead of offering assistance based on the functional limitations of one's disability.

Even worse for Sally, she seems to have fallen through the cracks of every social system that was designed to help her. It was not enough that Sally was functionally limited and could not work. She had to prove her worthiness for services, which meant having the right type of mental illness label to qualify for SSI. Being dependent on SSI in our culture can be a deeply diminishing experience. Many persons describe the system as one which "throws people away." The loss of functionality and the need to prove to a larger social system the legitimacy of your health condition make this an all too commonly negative experience for people who have led hard-working and productive lives up to the onset of their disability.

Clinical Interventions

1. Call an SSI representative by phone to discuss what actually occurred in Sally's case to cause her application to be denied.
2. Find out what paperwork needs to be added to her application.
3. Ask Sally's primary care physician to write a letter on Sally's behalf.
4. Encourage Sally to contact the neurologist that examined her to obtain a summary to add to her third application for SSI.
5. Empower Sally to represent her own point of view about what is wrong with the SSI system, exploring ways that she could intervene in a personal way to change the system. For example, write a letter to SSI representatives about what happened to her.
6. Allow Sally to assess how the larger social system has impacted her life to enable her to gain a different perspective and to feel less powerless.
7. Assist Sally in acknowledging the losses she has been experiencing, to discuss what they mean to her.
8. Address with Sally how she will function in her immediate home surroundings.
9. Address those physical barriers that exist and how she plans to make personal lifestyle changes in order to overcome them.
10. Acknowledge self-esteem issues that may be residual from making the transformation to a new lifestyle as a person with a disability.
11. Address how she is impacted by her new lifestyle and how she will respond to these challenges.
12. Work with Sally on controlling her stress response.
13. Discuss the triggers that led up to the suicide attempt, for example, filling out the application the third time.
14. Discuss with Sally how she can identify important persons to rely on in times of need, for example, friends and neighbors. Assist Sally with developing her own support network where she lives.
15. Acknowledge underlying anger issues, for example, what being labeled mentally ill means to her.
16. Address functional life issues as they arise; assist Sally with constructive strategies for solving her own problems.

Therapeutic Value

1. Validation of Sally's perceptions of the experiences and challenges she has encountered.
2. Validation of her sense of self and self-esteem as a person within the context of her transition.
3. Sally will begin to develop the belief that she can survive.
4. Sally will begin to acknowledge that she is a vital person even with her physical limitations and could in fact carve out a role in her life and community that could be functional and satisfying.
5. Sally will begin to acknowledge her strengths, abilities and interests, and find a way to live that brings about a sense of her own happiness.

20

Case: Barry

Co-author Peter Leech describes his interactions and insights about his work with this client.

Barry was referred to me for therapy after he had begun to live in a shelter for homeless men because everything had gone terribly wrong. He was also assigned to the drug treatment program in the area.

Barry, a white male, thirty-four years of age, had been under-employed for many years. His rage about this ultimately resulted in domestic violence, the break-up of his marriage, and separation from his children. As a result, Barry was placed on probation, was assigned to groups involved with anger management, and eventually reduced to living in a shelter.

For some time, Barry made attempts at participating in the groups but admitted that he did not finish any of them. His life continued to spiral downward because of his inability to find or keep employment. He acknowledged that he could not stay with any particular job because he had trouble fitting in socially with other co-workers, and did not understand what others were asking of him. From Barry's perspective, his real problem was that he needed to learn how to control himself better both from a social and religious standpoint.

My view of Barry's difficulties was quite different however. From where I sat, Barry had very serious memory deficits which affected how he operated. For example, he struggled and fretted anxiously about remembering important appointments. He showed up at my office door one day in a blind panic, thinking he didn't know when he was supposed to come to our meeting. He knocked on the office door loudly, interrupting me in a session with another client. I asked him if he had his wallet with him. He replied, "Oh yes, I have my wallet." At this, he got his wallet out and found that he still had the appointment card I had given him. Barry had not remembered to look in his wallet for the card in order to find out the appointment time. He could panic about not being there on time but had not made the connection that finding the appointment card might solve his problem. Barry seemed to lose focus easily when he was confronted with situations where he felt pressured to meet social expectations.

Barry was in contact with organizations that were trying to help him to get a job. At one of our meetings, he came in very excited and announced that he had just been to his first job in a long time. In the next sentence however, he announced that he had been evicted from the shelter because someone there said he had been smoking marijuana.

Barry did not question the account of the other person, nor agree with the story that he had been smoking marijuana. He just accepted the eviction without pressing or contesting the issue. Barry removed himself from the shelter and I did not hear where he was spending his nights from that time on.

Upon closer examination of Barry's general situation, I remembered that Barry had shared with me at an earlier time a very important fact. He had been a student in special education during his formative years and had been diagnosed with some with pretty significant learning disabilities. I didn't think about it at the time, but Barry had severe limitations, far more debilitating in the functional realm than anyone had probably realized. Barry recognized that he had trouble regulating his own behavior, but I had not realized that such difficulties taken in the context of a learning disability might mean that more significant life skill barriers existed.

Barry had significant life skill challenges having to do directly with integrating socially into the mainstream of society, following social rules and the social expectations of others. Most of us participate in our lives without having to think too much about remembering everything that is said to us.

I found myself asking over and over again, what were Barry's abilities? What were the disabilities that affected his functioning in the real world? How could I have sorted out the facts and assisted Barry with leading a more functional and productive life? What happens to individuals who graduate from high school having been in special education like Barry? Are they to be considered "special" forever? I always thought that they went on and did well in life, or do they? What is the truth about clients with invisible disabilities?

I admit it. I didn't know much about individuals like Barry. If Barry is any indication of the difficulties that many homeless people face out there, it is apparent to me that psychotherapists need to recognize this type of client because he is everywhere. We may already be dealing with individuals we normally think of as dysfunctional. Yet, these dysfunctional individuals operate within a whole dysfunctional social system filled with barriers that are hostile to their specific limitations.

Barry is no exception. The only recourse that Barry has is to continue to operate within his dysfunctional world trying to survive as best he can. As psychotherapists, we may feel as though we are too limited in our scope of expertise to assist with even a part of Barry's picture.

Yet Barry's needs are the same as other clients we serve. Barry needs to become more functional in his life, regardless of his disability.

Offering a lifeline to Barry is preferable to having him simply vanish into the margins of our consciousness. We all pay in little ways for those clients who do not succeed in society.

Our mental health focus is too inaccessible or non-applicable to the needs of this population. As I reflect upon what I know about Barry, I realize that he has overwhelming needs that surpass what I am able to provide as a psychotherapist. No one has made me a trained observer of Barry's disability. However, it was obvious from our first meeting that my approach to therapy needed to change.

I imagine that there are many psychotherapists who are dealing with learning disabled adults, yet do not recognize them as such. There are perhaps thousands that disappear into the folds of society every year. Perhaps they surface again and again like Barry without our direct notice.

Often they may appear in the center of our social service network confused or disoriented. We don't see immediately the invisible nature of their disabilities or ask enough questions. I have heard other therapists discard some clients as too violent, others as drug users, batterers, crazy, or worse, criminals deserving to spend time in our prisons. How many of them could be identified later as having a disability?

When I think about Barry's abilities to function with an eye to social expectations or job related tasks, I realize he could barely read, understand any paper process or comprehend what he heard others say to him.

Certainly he could not focus on an idea that we talked about for very long. How could he participate at all in anger management groups? Could he understand or even focus on what they were all talking about?

His puzzlement about certain words or statements I made now stands out to me because I took for granted that he could understand every word I said. I thought he had the ability to put ideas together so they made sense.

I now realize that he came to me with many limitations, a person without the abilities to fit comfortably into larger social systems. In fact, Barry did not have a clue about how to interface with them. His limitations obviously rubbed co-workers the wrong way and led to discomfort in all his relationships.

Barry's difficulties surfaced at some pretty basic levels of independent living. He did not communicate his needs or ask questions effectively. I remember how he would simply sit there and look blank if he did not understand me, or pretend that he did understand me. After he would ask questions that indicated that he had missed entirely what I had just been saying, I could only be amazed.

In short, I was dealing with a person with a very profound disability. His disability should be obvious to the observer after a few minutes of verbal exchange. But to look at him, no one would know it. You could not see the disability on him. Barry was learning disabled and unprepared for the world he was living in. How could I have bridged the gaps in Barry's life? What kind of help did Barry need?

Consultation and Approach to Client

Barry's situation shows the gross misunderstanding and confusion over the differences between disability and mental disorder. Barry's real problem was that he could not interface properly with any social system because of the functional limitations of his disability.

In fact, most social service agencies operate on the assumption that all persons have the ability to comply with organization requirements and should be able to figure the system out. When an adult having a severe disability tries to fit into the existing system, there is no label that will correctly fit the situation or indicate to agencies how persons like Barry should be served. In fact, social services are not designed to meet the needs of adults having extensive disability limitations. The assumption seems to be that adults with severe disabilities are taken care of by others, not living independently and managing their own lives.

Not even the best qualified therapist who knows about individuals with significant learning disabilities can anticipate what might be done in Barry's situation. It will continue to be a challenge for persons like Barry to access social services because the regulations only serve those people who are considered non-disabled or are labeled with the right mental disorder. It raises serious issues about who should be helping Barry to access the services he needs to survive and retain his independence and how that help should be given.

Another disturbing aspect of the challenges Barry faces has to do with the fact that any individual like Barry who behaves differently is automatically perceived by agency workers as noncompliant if the person is unable to adjust, adapt or comply within the social agency's expectations. The memory difficulties and inability on Barry's part to hold onto verbal information only adds to these perceptions, especially since his deficits would interfere with his abilities to participate in the programs he was required to attend, for example, the local drug prevention program.

Historically, one can look back and see that these same disability deficits would have interfered with his ability to finish school, or hold down a job, without some accommodations to help with those endeavors. Yet, individuals like Barry do survive, live among us all the time, managing to forge their own pathways that parallel the lives of persons without disabilities.

Clinical Interventions

Initially, it seems appropriate to work with Barry toward bringing an awareness of his learning deficits to the various agencies with which he is involved. This may mean interpreting and clarifying to the drug treatment program, the job service and the coordinator for the men's shelter what Barry's difficulties are, and what accommodations are required to make their particular programs useful to him. For example:

1. Encourage Barry to state what aspects of these programs are particularly difficult for him to participate in.
2. Work with programs on modifying their approach so that his disability limitations are considered and accommodations made in response so he can participate.
3. Assist these programs with working together to develop a comprehensive program approach that will enable Barry to experience success when he participates.
4. Work with probation (which assigned Barry to complete the anger management group) to set up an alternative program for Barry since the group was extremely auditory in nature, thus difficult for Barry to process.
5. Work individually with Barry toward his understanding both his strengths and functional limitations.
6. Begin a program to focus on his stress response, frustration level and anger.
7. Assist Barry in understanding how his limitations have impacted his current and past life experiences, and assist him with finding new ways to behave in adverse situations.
8. Address Barry's central goal or dream: something he wants bad enough to work toward making those behavioral changes that will ensure success.

Therapeutic Value

1. Barry will begin to experience himself as more successful and develop a framework to work within his abilities and strengths.
2. Barry will feel more confident in his ability to interact with larger social systems.
3. Barry will become more adept at developing more functional life skills to increase his level of overall independence.

21

Case: Tammy

Tammy was a forty-three-year-old woman who was referred for therapy and treatment of the acute stress she was experiencing while waiting to get started on a drug therapy program through the local mental health agency. She had been treated previously for bi-polar disorder by a psychiatrist, but had stopped because the drugs he had given her made her ill.

Having Hepatitis C only complicated matters further, as many of the medications taken for bi-polar increased the nausea brought on by the other condition. Shortly before coming to therapy, Tammy had been seeing a general practitioner in town who took her off all the medications she had been taking for reasons she was unsure of.

When Tammy arrived for therapy, she was in a manic phase of her bi-polar disorder and feeling edgy. She told the therapist that she thought her main problem was that she had been having a very hard time connecting with anyone at the mental health agency in order to get the medications she needed. As she talked it was difficult for the therapist to understand a picture of her history because she talked so fast. It was clear, however, that she was feeling very stressed and the therapist wanted to find a way to help Tammy.

Tammy explained that she had stopped drinking four years before when she was diagnosed with Hepatitis C and had begun to behave conscientiously around her health condition, controlling the temptations to drink. It was easy, according to Tammy, to stop her habit because she did not feel well a lot of the time.

In the absence of Tammy's drinking, however, her other mental health difficulties surfaced and became noticeable. Tammy went through periods of mania and severe depression. Desperate to find out what was wrong with her, Tammy had contacted a mental health professional in the area where she then lived who diagnosed her with bi-polar disorder. Tammy continued to abstain from drinking, also taking medications to relieve the symptoms.

The therapist continued to meet with Tammy over the course of six weeks. The main focus was reducing her stress level so that she could sleep at night. The ongoing issue seemed to be, however, accessing the medications she needed to control her bi-polar condition.

Tammy had twice been refused services at the mental health agency. To Tammy's way of thinking, she should qualify for their services since she had a report containing a diagnosis of a mental disorder. She agreed with the therapist that she should now go back and speak again with the agency about what she needed.

For a third time Tammy approached the local mental health agency and was refused services. She showed her confidential reports to counselors and demanded to know why she had been rejected again. The counselors responded to the question this time. Tammy had a history of drinking and, because she had admitted that she had used other drugs in the past, the agency was taking the position that they could not supply her with drugs of any kind. In their minds, Tammy's real problem was that she had a drug problem and needed help from the drug treatment program in the area. They refrained from commenting on the fact she had a diagnosis for which medications seemed necessary and appropriate.

The mental health agency sent Tammy away, recommending that she contact the drug treatment program for help. Tammy had a hard time understanding how admitting to her past drug problems had interfered with her chances to receive services from the mental health agency. Apparently, clients are referred to substance abuse treatment programs if they currently have or have had any drug related problems, regardless of the history of mental disorder.

Tammy's anger went deeper than that. She was told by the mental health counselor that she needed to be considered alcohol dependent even though she had been clean and sober for four years. It was apparent that Tammy's history with alcohol and drugs was more important to the mental health agency counselors than looking at Tammy's actual manic behavior. The therapist wondered if either program, the mental health agency or drug treatment program, were educated in working with dual diagnoses.

Consultation and Approach to Client

Tammy's dilemma was that she had two separate health conditions: Hepatitis C and bi-polar disorder. It is true that Tammy also had a history of addiction but for Tammy this was not a current issue to be addressed as the most salient factor in her eligibility for agency services. Although the agencies had a heavy emphasis on diagnostic labeling, Tammy's was excluded from services on the basis of not having just the right diagnosis to fit neatly into the standards each agency required. And like Sally's case, even though it was clear that Tammy required attention from the professionals, the labels did not serve to bring her closer access to the services she really needed.

Local mental health agencies around the country are designed and funded to be responsive to those individuals diagnosed with mental illness (such as Tammy's). Ironically, the very policies and practices designed to assist with case management of Tammy's mental disorder also created barriers to Tammy getting the appropriate treatment for her condition because her past history indicated that she was a drug user. Because Tammy was labeled by the local mental health agency as a drug user, she was denied on that basis with suggestions that she be served by another local community agency that specifically deals with drug users.

But meeting the eligibility standards of each agency was not the only problem Tammy had in getting served in her community. The agencies did not seem to recognize or want to deal with the potential issue of dual diagnosis. The negative attitude and accompanying assumptions on the part of agency workers to Tammy's situation only added to the system barriers Tammy was experiencing. The local mental health agency made three assumptions about Tammy's situation:

1. "Once a drug user, always a drug user."
2. If you have a drug problem of any kind, you must be treated by a drug program not a mental health program.
3. Persons with dual diagnoses like Tammy's are not recognized as eligible for mental health program services.

Clinical Interventions

1. Make a joint telephone call, with Tammy, to the psychiatrist who made the diagnosis of bi-polar to request that (with Tammy's permission) he provide a current statement of Tammy's condition, outlining the need for medications and support services, to you as her current clinician.
2. Arrange with Tammy to have this information transmitted to Mental Health prior to making a phone call to this agency.
3. Establish a working relationship with Mental Health that would recognize joint efforts to stabilize Tammy and move toward a unified approach that might take into account her dual diagnosis.

4. Address the fact that the drug program also has guidelines which could restrict serving Tammy, since such clients are viewed as mental health clients.
5. Assist Tammy in becoming her own advocate. Involve Tammy in planning and contacting agency personnel in her own behalf.
6. Continue to work with Tammy around her individual issues of functioning in everyday living and adjustment to her illnesses, bipolar and Hepatitis C.

Therapeutic Value

1. Reduction of Tammy's stress level so that she can sleep better.
2. Increase of Tammy's overall functionality within her immediate social surroundings.
3. Increase of Tammy's level of self-esteem, satisfaction and personal fulfillment.

22

Case: Max

Max, an African-American man of approximately 47 years of age, was referred for therapy. He had been transient and homeless most of his adult life.

Early in his childhood, Max could remember his parents fighting. Home life was filled with uncertainty and unpredictable events that rocked his sense of security. At age seven his parents separated. His brothers and sisters were divided into separate households. Although he tried to understand this event, his adjustment was poor.

Throughout the next few years, Max craved the support of fully functioning parents. In school he was verbally endowed with an excellent vocabulary, retained a lot of what he was able to hear in the classroom but lacked the ability to express himself in writing. Because he grew up before the special education law was passed in 1975, he was not formally diagnosed with a learning disability.

Max described his teen years as tumultuous. He became involved with drugs and alcohol to cover up the pain of feeling like a social misfit. He ended his experimentation with drugs and alcohol by the time he turned twenty-one.

During his teens, however, he sustained multiple head injuries in accidents resulting in lost consciousness. From those incidents, Max began to struggle with memory limitations. His ability to retain information diminished as a result of the head injuries.

Getting and keeping employment was a major challenge because he did not respond appropriately to conflict. In fact, Max showed a distinct intolerance for authority figures. In each new job setting he responded to the pressures placed on him by simply leaving the situation behind. For Max, disappearing was the only alternative to confrontation.

When Max was thirty-five, he experienced an incident that changed his life. Police severely beat him because of suspected drug abuse. This traumatic run-in with the police resulted in Max receiving therapy and treatment from a psychiatrist for post-traumatic stress disorder. Through this relationship with his psychiatrist, Max was able to obtain SSI.

After the traumatic incident Max described himself as a wanderer moving in and out of jobs. He fled from place to place fearing that the police would attack him again. This became the pattern whenever Max feared that he could not meet social expectations.

At age forty-four he met a woman who was also homeless and on SSI because of her own emotional difficulties. The woman had both African-American and Caucasian heritage. She was very light skinned and was, if she chose to, able to pass for white. Max and the woman, Jane, hit it off together. They decided to pool their resources and move into a "fixer upper house" together. Because he was so creative with his hands, Max was able to turn the house into a functional living space for the two of them.

Not too much time went by before Jane discovered she was pregnant. She did not react well to the news. She became distraught, attempting suicide more than once. Max did his best to help Jane in her emotional state. He nursed her through the pregnancy and it seemed as though everything would be all right again. The baby was born healthy at nine months gestation. Max was enamored of the new baby. But the stress of having a new baby, the sleep deprivation and the shortage of funds took its toll on the two of them. Their conflict became habitual. Max was asked by Jane to leave the house several times. He would leave for a time and then return. Heated arguments continued.

On the day the baby they called Zoey was turning two years old, Jane insisted that Max leave the home to find his own place. For a time Jane allowed Max to continue to visit Zoey on a fairly regular basis. This was followed by the move of Jane's mother into the area, near Jane and Zoey's house. With the support of Jane's mother who was now living nearby, Jane decided that she no longer wanted to associate with Max.

In the next few weeks, Jane decided to give up the house she and Max had lived in to move in with her mother. Jane and her mother decided that they together would raise Zoey. Because Jane's mother was white and Jane could pass for white, she wanted to sever the ties completely with Max. Jane wanted to raise her daughter free from his black ancestry.

In order to facilitate such a complete separation, Jane hired an attorney and filed a complaint that Max had been physically threatening to her. With the filing of this complaint, the situation entered the legal system.

Max found himself being accosted by the police. At one point he was taken to jail because Jane happened to be at the same store as he. The restraining order she had obtained was enforced. She stated to the policeman that Max had come to the store to harass her and her daughter Zoey.

Although Max explained his position to the policeman, the policeman had no recourse because of the structure of the law. He had to arrest Max. Because of this incident the issue of Jane's desire for custody and the idea of child endangerment entered the court system for the first time.

Jane approached the local women's shelter as a woman who had been abused by her husband, although she had never approached this agency for any reason before. She sought and received the support and attention she expected to find. Because of the story that Jane told, Max was viewed as a dangerous father who would stop at nothing to hurt his ex-wife. Jane created the illusion with these agencies that she had been wronged and threatened by Max. She further convinced them that her daughter, Zoey, needed to be protected as well.

The case went to court. Without further investigation, the court judge ruled that Max could not visit his daughter without being in a supervised setting, even though there was no evidence brought forth to indicate why supervision would be required around his daughter, Zoey.

Also, the battered women's shelter was asked by the judge to oversee the supervision of Max's visits with Zoey. At this, Max became extremely upset, angry that his role as a father was being usurped. He was also growing increasingly agitated, confused and distraught over the false accusations and the lack of representation in the legal system to protect his rights.

Max could not think of anywhere to go with his side of the story. He decided that he needed to confer with the local mental health agency about his particular dilemma. Mental Health did not approach his situation with sympathy. The counselor told Max that in essence, he needed to accept the fact that he could no longer see his daughter.

Discouraged by the message he was getting from Mental Health, Max approached a therapist for emotional support. He also was asking for assistance with finding an attorney to represent the legal ramifications of his case.

With the finding of an attorney who would represent Max, the case was further polarized into separate camps. Max had been allowed to visit his daughter with more open visit times; for example, Max could take the child to the park and bring her back to the shelter after a few hours. Jane did not like this at all. She contested the open visits with accusations that Max was using drugs and drugging his child. Jane convinced the counselors at the shelter that this must be true because Zoey appeared sleepy when Jane picked her up. This accusation was brought to the attention of the court judge.

Drug testing was ordered by the judge. Neither Max nor Zoey tested positive for drugs. The results were ignored. The judge ordered Max to receive complete supervision during visits with Zoey. Mental Health was asked to conduct an evaluation to determine the mental state of Max on behalf of the court. Mental Health stated that they were unable to provide such an evaluation. Another clinician was ordered to provide a Mental Health evaluation for the court.

The evaluation took place and the results did not work in Max's favor. He was described in court as having an anti-social type disorder. The evaluator also stated that Max would benefit from personal counseling and parenting classes. The mental health evaluator was struck by the intensity of Max's anger and warned of its implications in the context of child rearing.

The judge agreed with the findings that Max should receive personal counseling, attend parenting classes and participate in anger management groups. Max wondered why Jane was not questioned for her mental health and fitness as a parent. The cards seemed stacked against Max. No one questioned Jane's veracity.

Max's attorney was contacted to see if he could provide some idea of the real nature of the legal situation and to inquire if the court was not ignoring positive aspects of Max's involvement with Zoey. It had already been established that Max was not using drugs, nor exposing Zoey to them. Max's attorney stated that there was nothing he could do.

Max chafed under the lack of justice. He stated his belief to anyone who would listen that there was no justification for Jane's accusations and that he had complied with all the judge's requests. He also complained that his rights as a father were being subjugated to the belief that Jane was "totally in the right" and he was "totally in the wrong." He now found himself caught up in a legal system that was unreceptive to his plight, his attorney's fees mounting even though it was known that he had virtually no income to support himself on. Even worse, the legal representation was inadequate. In short, Max had most of his opportunities to maintain contact with his daughter taken from him, and was being viewed as an unfit father.

What could the therapist do to help Max?

Consultation and Approach to Client

In reviewing this case, it was obvious that the diagnostic label of mental disorder hung in the air over Max's head like a dark cloud. It was used time and again as the primary reason to deny Max his visitation rights and access to his daughter. Had his ex-wife not been able to use the label to her advantage in court, the issue surrounding Max as an unfit father may never have been raised in the first place.

Max had more than his share of bad experiences due to inappropriate labeling however. Community agencies aligned themselves with either parent on the basis of the label and what they believed to be true about Max. None of the community professionals worked effectively together for the needs of the child or enabled the parents to work together in any meaningful way.

The mental health agency, for example, openly stated to Max that he must forget his dream of having a daughter in his life which was, in effect, assuming that Max was in the wrong all along. The attorneys were too heavily invested in whatever legal steps must be taken next. Both sides seem to have conflicting realities of what actually occurred between Max and Jane. The court case lagged on with the judge making new requests for Max to prove that he was a fit father.

As a result of the confusion stemming from Max's diagnosis, the judge finally decided that Max must be observed and evaluated for his mental fitness by a local therapist that both sides could agree on. Deciding what mental health reports and other supportive documentation should be admissible in court became an ongoing issue that slowed the court case down, possibly from ever being completely resolved.

Clinical Interventions

1. Acknowledge and validate Max's sense of loss, frustration and fear that his intention to be a positive father figure in his daughter's life is being undermined and diminished.
2. Set up a meeting with the local women's shelter and the lawyers to begin focus on the ostensible goal, which should be to get this family to work together around the needs of the child.
3. Inquire from the judge whether an impartial professional mediation entity might be able to meet with both sides to develop a strategy to move forward outside of court.
4. Motivate Max to be his own change agent, to self-advocate, asserting himself to make his viewpoint known to others. Many popular ways of raising visibility to the issue include utilizing newspapers, radio stations, TV newscasts, the internet, contact local chapters for advocacy groups such as the American Civil Liberties Union, etc.
5. Because Max has difficulties expressing himself on paper (due to his learning disability), encourage Max to use a tape recorder to record his side of the story which could then be utilized by his attorney, or to provide a copy to potential civil rights organizations he contacts for support.

6. Encourage Max to become involved with support groups for single fathers, families and other advocacy groups. Fathers who are involved with similar parent-child rights issues can provide another perspective as well as other resources for Max to tap into.
7. Encourage Max to evaluate the effectiveness of the legal representation he has received thus far, and perhaps determine if better legal representation is available. If so, assist with the search for a new attorney to represent his case.
8. Focus individual therapy on how to channel Max's anger in a more pro-active mode so that he is putting his energies into solving his problem rather than feeling victimized by system barriers where certainly he has limited control.
9. Present Max with the option of contacting his local legislators about what has happened to his case and the lack of justice that he is experiencing within the community and justice system.

Therapeutic Value

1. Supporting Max in a therapeutic alliance will help him by validating his sense of himself as a father.
2. Supporting Max's goal of being a positive father in his daughter's life will help motivate him to develop the skills he needs to more effectively work with the social systems from which he feels so alienated.
3. Working with Max around focusing the energy behind his feelings in a positive effort toward systems change will further demonstrate his intention to be a positive force in his daughter's life.

Myth IV

The System of Diagnostic Labeling Provides Solutions to Social Problems

Introduction: The Ultimate Betrayal

CASE ILLUSTRATION

Mr. Bill Jamison walked from his office to his car. He had conducted a private practice doing psychotherapy for thirty-five years. Pulling the letter out of his pocket and re-reading its contents, he sighed, looked at his pocket watch, and unlocked the car door.

"How could it come to this?" he wondered. His world had turned around in a twenty-four-hour period. His private practice could dissolve. He would now be required to comply with new regulations imposed on him by the federal and state governments. Referrals of clients could no longer be made to him unless he was willing to work within the confines of the clinic's facility. Bill had not worked for anyone else for quite some time. His fingers twitched as he nervously put the letter in his pocket and proceeded to drive home.

Seated at the dinner table that night with his wife, Marge, he stared straight ahead, as if in a fog, before retrieving the letter. Marge had prepared a sweet-smelling pot roast with scalloped potatoes and cut asparagus. She was also preparing herself for what she sensed was something huge in their lives that had landed in the room between the two of them. A life changing event was happening and it was somehow connected to

Bill's work situation, but what? With the same casual air as she had done for thirty years, she placed his favorite glass of Port next to a plate containing a single slice of Brie cheese on the table at his place.

Bill opened the crumpled letter and began to read the words aloud:

April 20, 2006

Dear Psychotherapist:

Beginning June 11, all therapists who accept referrals from New Havens will be required to see patients in the two facilities on the main campus of New Havens Mental Health Services. There will be full or part-time positions available to those therapists who are interested in being employed by our agency. For those therapists who are employed, or those therapists who choose to continue their contracts, office space will be provided where clients can be met on site. Those therapists who work part-time will be required to use the available rooms and to share office space with other therapists. Therapists are expected to arrange their own hours with other therapists. Giving the limited availability of therapy rooms, therapists are encouraged to make their needs known to the administrative staff at the earliest possible time to ensure space availability.

If you are interested in an employee position, please submit to our office the following items by May 15:

1. Cover letter outlining your interest in the position
2. A completed application form
3. Current CV and the credentialing packet that you received at our last meeting.

PLEASE NOTE: PER FEDERAL REGULATIONS ALL LICENSED PROFESSIONALS WHO PROVIDE MENTAL HEALTH SERVICES TO PATIENTS REFERRED BY THIS CLINIC MUST COMPLY WITH THE COMPLETE MENTAL HEALTH AGENCY PROTOCOL.

All applications will be reviewed by the head administrative staff and individual appointments will be made for interview and further discussion of the positions.

Salary will be based on the level of Clinician experience, not to exceed $38.00 per hour. The administration understands that this is far from competitive professional pay for most clinicians in private practice, however, this agency is experiencing significant financial difficulties and thus, can not afford a higher fee for services at this time.

If you are not interested in an employee position with our agency but still wish to continue to receive referrals from this agency, please communicate your intentions to me by May 15, 2006.

NOTE: CONTRACTORS ARE REQUIRED TO SEE PATIENTS ON SITE AT EITHER OF NEW HAVEN'S MENTAL HEALTH FACILITIES.

Therapists not interested in continuing to receive referrals from this agency, please submit a letter to me by May 15 indicating your intent and your decision.

I look forward to hearing from you.

Sincerely, Dr. Latisha Clark

Quiet reigned in the room for a moment. Marge gasped, "Oh my stars!" She sat down abruptly in a chair across from Bill at the table.

Bill looked up and said, "You heard it right, Marge. It could cut my hourly fees by forty percent. It's a disgrace, but you haven't heard the worst of it. All my patients will be run through a lot of tedious paperwork with the insurance programs dictating what therapists will need to put down on paper so these people can be served. Bureaucrats in Washington are now in the business of telling us how therapy ought to be conducted in all these private rooms at New Havens if we wish to be paid! It won't be doing psychotherapy any more, but a way that the damned government can track all these poor people and make sure they really need the money for therapy. I interpret this to mean that therapists will be under some kind of pressure, or at least encouraged, to come up with diagnoses that are severe enough, damaging enough, to qualify in the minds of insurance people. To them, it's all about who gets, who doesn't. It's not about people getting their lives back together. The idea of having all these poor people run through a paper mill that gives each one a diagnosis of some sort of god-awful mental illness makes my skin crawl. Before too long, the government is going to be in the business of telling us which labels we ought to be giving to these people, as if they don't have enough of bad times as it is! And there isn't going to be any oversight. No oversight of these so-called insurance people doing late night reading of all the private progress notes. Oh no, it will be we therapists who are accused of impropriety when things are not done right. We should be grateful enough for income. Isn't that what a government job is for!?"

Marge did not know what to say so she decided the best thing to do at a time like this was to settle down in her chair and listen, and not offer Bill a second glass of Port.

Bill could not sit down long enough to drink a glass of Port. Instead, he stood up and said "I'm going for a walk. I'm sorry Marge, I don't feel like eating right now, but if you put a plate for me in the fridge, I would love a bite when I get back. It smells terrific, really." With that, Bill got up from the table, grabbed his jacket and was gone through the door.

"That was that," Marge muttered to herself. But she wondered, "What would happen to all these poor people under the new system? Is it true that all these people would be given some sort of mental illness label?" Marge cleared the dishes off the table and drank the glass of Port herself. "No," she thought. This is something much different from anything she had imagined. The worst of it was not about Bill's clients, but what was happening to Bill. She slumped down in the big chair to read the paper.

Bill walked down to the edge of the vacant lot that separated his house from the county park a little distance away. The ethics of doing business as usual had changed. The world for his clients lives had changed. It no longer came down to saving his clients. He was the one who had to fight for his own survival as a professional. His income was dependent upon the referrals made to him by New Havens. He now had to comply with the new agency requirements or face a decline in referrals. His income would be diminished significantly without those referrals. Private pay clients were scarce. There was no point in starting a private practice in another part of the state. He was too old to consider a different career. What did the new system really mean? When you get right down to it, there would be predictable referrals, predictable hours, predictable pay, and the fact that when clients don't show up for their appointments, he would still get paid by the agency. Was it all that bad? he wondered.

It was more than that he knew. But why were the other therapists not all up in arms like he was? What is it about this whole thing that is so disturbing? He thought about how he felt the first time a client came to his new office years ago. It had been a comfortable space, a humble arrangement, not terribly large. Nothing fancy, a couple of pillows arranged on a couch in an eight by ten room. There was nothing about New Havens that was particularly demeaning to clients. Perhaps a little hospital-like, but he could warm the room with some photos or art. The problem wasn't the fact that he had to share office space with others. He had done that before in other towns. What was it?

The tone of the letter was disturbing to him. He was being ordered to take part in what was necessary for the agency to be in compliance with the state and federal government. He felt no particular allegiance to New Havens. They were just a mental health agency that provided referrals to him, nothing more. Now he had been asked to join them, no, ordered to join, to comply with the law. What law? Who made the law? Who was it who had the upper hand over his private practice? No one had told him since he got his license thirty years ago that someday it would mean giving up his freedoms as a private practicing therapist. Now there was a new movement afoot. Was it set up to control therapists? Didn't the other therapists question this at all? What sort of interpretations were they coming up with, he wondered? Did they care about the ethical side of this whole affair?

Bill thought about the fact that some therapists would split away from New Havens. They were the ones who had large practices of private-pay clients. Wealthy clients, of course, could keep paying their own fees. They would be untouched by the new system. He had that choice, but Bill realized he had chosen to work in the trenches most of his life with clients no one else would serve. Why he thought, did I choose this type of client? Did low income clients deserve more of his time? Was there some personal need he had to serve this population? Or was it that other therapists refused to have them as clients? This always bothered him. "The country is made up of the average Joe Blow," he said to himself out loud. It does not matter if the person is homeless, low income, or the color green. He had served them all well. His office was filled with small tokens and gifts from clients who were grateful for his involvement in their lives. He had given them a new lease on their lives and they had wanted him to know how important that was to them.

And now his world was changing because of a new law. Bill clenched his fists. The government was becoming more like Big Brother every day, it seemed. Why was he being asked to compromise his ethics, his private practice, just to get paid for low-income clients who had the misfortune of needing government-sponsored (Medicare or Medicaid) insurance?

Bill did not sleep well. He woke up in the night thinking about his clients. This is outrageous, he thought. The insurance companies were in control of his business. The lives of his clients would be forever altered, but they had no clue how. How would they feel and what would they do if they were told that they had to be labeled mentally disordered and have their personal information fed into state and federal computer systems in order for them to be treated? In the sixties, this sort of thing would have been called institutionalized discrimination against the poor. He was participating in something that set these people apart from others. He might get through this ordeal himself, but it would mean harming the very people who had instilled their trust in him. This did not feel right. It was not right. He would be violating his own professional standards to serve these clients under this new system. Didn't other therapists see this? Why weren't they taking a stronger stand to protect themselves and their clients' rights? Aren't we supposed to be the ones to protect, support, and advocate for the underdog? What were insurance companies doing in psychotherapy anyway? Who made them the overseer to decide how a psychotherapist should label clients? Were the people at the insurance helm licensed like he was? How did they come to make such important decisions in the lives of his clients? They didn't even know who his clients were! It was an outrage.

Eventually Bill did fall asleep, but it was not restful sleep. He dreamed that his clients revolted. There was a great rumbling in his yard. They were appearing in great numbers. All of his clients over the last thirty-five years were gathered outside his bedroom demanding their rights. He could see their faces from his window. He watched in amazement as they picketed in a circle. Pretty soon they crossed over the vacant lot from everywhere carrying signs and yelling. They were angry and demanding the return of their files! One person threw a rock at his bedroom window and missed him narrowly. Pretty soon, they were all getting into the act, picking up stones and heaving them at the bedroom window.

Bill awakened with a start and sat up. Marge also woke up and stared at her husband who had leaped out of bed and slammed the opened window down. He then got into his robe and sat down on the bed next to her. He said to Marge in a low tone of voice, "Marge, I have to do something. I don't know what it is, but I have to do something." Marge nodded and said, "Does it have to be right now?"

The next morning Bill sat thumbing through the professional journals. He was thinking about all the new approaches to treatment that he had heard and read about recently. How could any of these new approaches be effective in this new system? *What have we wrought?* was the name of one of the articles. Humh, yes, "What have we wrought?" he asked of himself. Today would be a day like any other day, he thought. He would not think about the new system today. He would go to his office and meet with clients. What would he tell them about the transfer to New Havens?

Two weeks was all he had to make up his mind. Then in another month or so, he was expected to hand the keys of his life back to the landlord of his office space and tell the friend with whom he had had coffee every Monday morning for the last fifteen years that he wouldn't be doing Mondays anymore after June 1st. Sadly, Bill looked at himself in the mirror. He needed a good shave. He began to feel queasy as he thought about the night before; about the state and federal governments having a hand in his private world, his clinical world, the world he was fond of, a world of integrity where a license and experience meant something. What business was it of the government to interfere with his professional domain, his ability to make clinical decisions in the best interest of his clients? How could he look in the faces of so many clients and at the same time be an informant for governmental entities. He would be expected to disclose to other unknown people that so and so had a mental illness. What if they didn't have mental illness, then what? Bill shuddered. And for what purpose should he be in the position of providing mental health counseling to someone, just to satisfy a social services worker? Just the other day a client had come to him explaining that Social Services required her to have therapy in order to qualify for a subsidy for housing from HUD. Wasn't that the craziest thing he had heard of? What were they supposed to talk about? What kind of label would he have to come up with under this new system so that she would get a home? Everyone was required to have a label. This is absurd. Bill was angrier now than he was last night. Really angry now! But what could he do? Who was responsible for the injustice? What did it all mean? What sort of ethical breaches would he have to traverse?

Bill couldn't take one more sleepless night and called his friend Jim, a practicing psychiatrist in the area.

Jim answered the phone and was surprised that his friend Bill was on the other end of the receiver and talking almost inaudibly at 2:00 PM in the afternoon. Bill sounded fragile, his voice slightly frayed, cracking when he stated Jim's name. "Bill is distraught," Jim thought.

"Well Bill, what's going on, my friend?"

Bill sighed and stated in a more composed fashion, "Jim, I need to come see you. There is a problem with my work situation, or my loss of a referral base, whatever you call it, and I may have to move from my office into another agency facility. I don't really understand what these damned state regulations are talking about, but I realize that it is inevitable and I don't know which way to turn. My life has turned upside down. I can't sleep and when I do, I have bad dreams. For the last two weeks I haven't been able to eat well and I am losing weight.

"I need some help from you, maybe some therapy, but I can't have anyone find out about this. I will pay you of course, for three visits only, that's all, I don't want to find myself with some goddamned label for life, plastered across my forehead, the subject of ridicule would almost be worse than litigation. Think of my clients. They do deserve someone more together than I am right now."

Jim offered to prescribe Zoloft, but Bill declined.

Bill responded by thinking a moment, taking a gulp of air, then stated: "No, I don't want any drugs! I want to see you and talk to you and resolve some of these bad feelings in my gut. Something has really taken hold of me and I can't concentrate because of what has happened.

"I'd like to meet with you on Sunday afternoon because I don't want anyone to know I am coming to your office on anything other than a casual basis. If the other therapists knew I was in trouble, what would be said around town? How about my clients? It doesn't really feel right to me that they might see that I am receiving therapy at the same time that I am seeing them as my clients, if you know what I mean. The word could get out there and pretty soon my practice is being questioned by fledglings twenty years my junior. I can't afford to take any flak right now. I need to get my life back into gear where I feel more in control of things again."

Jim agreed to the arrangement to having their first session on Sunday afternoon.

Session 1: Week One

Jim greeted Bill, showed him to a chair, and offered him a cup of coffee. Jim was uncomfortable meeting with his old friend under such circumstances and it took him a few minutes to get into the psychiatrist's mode. He turned to Bill and said in a rather nervous and awkward fashion, "So, Bill, tell me what changes are happening at New Havens."

Bill sputtered, "I have to get rid of my office, of all things, and move to their facility! I can't believe this is happening to me after all these years! I've always maintained my own comfortable space. The more relaxed environment of my personal space kind of conveys who I am as a psychotherapist, the way I think about things, and is designed to try to put clients at ease. I have artwork, comfortable chairs, and a confidential situation, within which they can do the work they need to do. And most of the therapists I've talked to have similar thoughts. They want to continue to work with clients who have been referred through this agency, but to have to travel over to a renovated, sterile building to see people in rather stark, depersonalized treatment rooms is not an appealing prospect."

"So is it that the atmosphere would be demeaning to you, or more of a business approach than you like?" Jim was now assuming a more professional demeanor toward Bill.

"Well it would certainly be a contrast to the kind of atmosphere that somebody who has private insurance or a private-pay person would want to be a part of. The basic message to the average client who had been in my office space and then would be required to revert back to the other facility would be that they are patients in the low pay clinic situation, therefore they get low pay facilities. It also implies to me, that if I work with a client in my private office and get paid through some federal or state insurance program that I am taking unfair advantage of public money."

Jim asked Bill to focus more clearly on what the issue really is for him. Bill thought for several minutes, then answered.

"The requirement to operate under the auspices of an agency diminishes the value of my professional education, experience, and licensing. The integrity of my making appropriate professional decisions because I understand my clients' needs, is diminished by having to kow-tow to an impersonal labeling system for the needs of an insurance company, in which the needs of my client and real struggles get left by the wayside. I now have to weigh my clients' needs toward recovery next to the punitive label they are given and develop treatment goals that are aligned with the labels which will be sent to the insurance programs instead of designing programs that reflect the actual issues. The insurance programs are not going to care about the needs of my clients the way I do.

"I feel diminished under the federal regulations to have to see myself and others go through some new special order to match agency protocols in order to satisfy where the money comes from to get paid for any of the work I do with clients. It seems more like a surveillance system you might expect of another country. I feel the distrust of the government, that somehow I am using that money to pad my own pocket and it bothers me. It's as though I don't have any ethics, and my clients are not due any respect at all."

Jim commented that maybe this is the cost of doing business these days.

Bill continued, "And as the so called 'psychotherapist licensed to practice privately,' I am being watched to make sure that I don't cheat anyone in my private office! Do you know that the assistant director is even talking about holding a workshop to show all the private therapists how to write 'treatment goals' that will be acceptable to the insurance companies?" Bill's fingers twitched as he made a gesture indicating his sarcasm. "Imagine that! As if, somehow, the insurance programs need to muddy the waters further by imposing their own control over the paperwork therapists submit to the mother system. What the hell is the government doing in bed with the insurance programs in the first place? What am I being programmed to do with poor people? This is all about social control, not the client's issues."

Jim seemed a little unnerved at this, but encouraged Bill to continue to talk further. Bill proceeded with:

"Jim, you know I was in the service and after I got out I went to school, got my degrees, and really wanted to help people with their problems. Not even a medal in the Navy compares to the pride I felt when I received my license to practice privately with clients. I don't even recognize this new system where everyone has to have a label, and can never get fixed. No one really talks about the ethical decisions that need to be made and the seriousness of the effect on people's lives. In the last ten–fifteen years it has all changed. It's become a business of a different nature. In contrast to being committed to caring for the client, it has become caring for the government regulations and complying with the governmental regulations, rather than the professional considerations.

"The state licensing boards are supposed to be designed to protect the consumers. They have been kind of taken out of the loop. It seems now that it is a national credentialing board that is doing their work, and state agencies have to now operate according to the regulations proposed by the federal government in order to stay in medical insurance programs, and the licensing boards don't seem to have much to do with it. On the other hand, from the perspective of people being labeled as mentally ill it seems that the consumer protection mantle under which licensing boards operate now seems rather loose because of the need to encourage therapists to follow the DSM-IV track, instead of recognizing the ethical breaches that can take place at the client's expense. The whole issue of providing a label just to perpetuate a business based on the arbitrary practice of labeling seems inconsistent with the training I have received and the code of ethics, especially as regards providing more severe diagnoses so that they are acceptable for re-imbursement purposes."

Bill shook his head and wrung his hands. "It seems unclear to me anymore. It would seem to me that consumers should have the right to know that the person they are working with is a qualified professional that would operate within ethical guidelines. To not hold the client's interests as primary is foreign to me. To not consider how clients function as the focus of therapy, but as secondary to other business considerations is more than I can take." Bill wept.

Jim could see that Bill was upset. He turned to his appointment book and scheduled a time for the following week.

Session 2: Week Two

Bill opened the session by stating he'd been doing more thinking about the subject of ethics and his training.

"Just like you, I had to study and learn about ethics and ways to work with people from a wide range of backgrounds, many of them oppressed. The code of ethics was big when I was in training. It was like, well, being in the Navy, I guess. There was a right way and a wrong way to do things, to show your respect, to conduct yourself in the way that commanded respect from others. You had a commander who led the way but you were also encouraged to respect yourself and the other people you worked with. You were always looking out for the welfare of others aside from yourself. My deepest sense of pride was upholding certain principles that I believe in today, such the 'do no harm' principles. Those ethics exist for a good reason. Without them, people get hurt.

"What really gets to me is that in this day and age it seems that a psychotherapist is expected to be nothing more than a technician. It used to be that a therapist had to have more experience, understanding of ethics, and practical knowledge accrued in order to be able to work flexibly, creatively and effectively with the variations in human thought and behavior, and kinds of problems presented. Few, if any, of my colleagues remember what it was like before the DSM-IV system arrived, just twelve years ago! Those that do seem to take it for granted without any sense of concern. Previous to that, diagnosis was based on the circumstances of a client's life, and the client's strengths that could be mobilized to resolve their difficulty. The idea that this can be boiled down to, or rendered in simplified form, so that the psychotherapist is, from the governmental point of view, simply a technician that applies a diagnosis and then provides service on the basis of the diagnosis, guts or eviscerates the very essence of psychotherapy.

"It is the depersonalized nature of it that I disagree with. It all seems to be headed toward treatment by diagnosis, medical model stuff.

"I believe that the goals I set with clients should be based on what they are experiencing as well as the challenges in their immediate social environment. A diagnosis should not take on a life of its own. Take me, for example. I feel like one of those people that got stuck in a hurricane. I feel like my life has been blown apart. Coming to you, the very last thing I want is for you to tell me that I'm just depressed because I can't eat or sleep. If you put it down that I'm clinically depressed, nothing else is going to be said about my life circumstances. The real problem will never get addressed. I'm going to be seen as clinically depressed, rather than someone who just lost everything that was important to me. Well I have seen the faces of people who got stuck in the hurricane, lost their house and everything in it, and have been displaced. Imagine what you or I would feel if we woke up in Houston, rather than New Orleans. It could be you or me. You can see, can't you, Jim, how we might be having some trouble sleeping at night?

"The most egregious thing is the idea of trying to get related to a client's inner thoughts and feelings while outside the door someone is banging on it saying hurry up! Hearing in the back room, 'Will you get this diagnosis done?' Get this client fixed because there is someone else waiting in the assembly line! All this happening while I am trying to listen carefully to what the client is actually saying is like having someone revving up a lawn mower outside the window. And all the nuances of human interaction and behavior, the kind of things spoken of and paid attention to over the years of training that have become second nature to me, are now seen as unnecessary fluff. I can't establish a sense of privacy and trust when we are sitting in a treatment room where you can hear everything that is in the other four treatment rooms around.

"The psychotherapeutic process of today seems diminished and not to value any of the background or experience of the psychotherapist; it doesn't matter about what you think anymore. What we are concerned about here is a DSMMD diagnosis and I believe that puts a client at risk because it diminishes the freedom and flexibility I have to really get related to what is going on in the lives of my clients, and to be effective and helpful where I can be."

Jim seemed uncomfortable with this idea, but Bill went on.

"I just heard from some colleagues who had returned from a conference. They talked a blue streak about all the good things that are happening in the field right now, the evolution of psychotherapy, and even a refocus on what constitutes mental health. But when I raised the questions of whether those kinds of promises could happen in this type of psychotherapeutic environment, with all the agency requirements and regimens around adhering to governmental policies, the reaction was one of dismay. I told them that my concern is that in today's therapy room there won't be any opportunity to use innovative approaches because it's all about matching agency requirements and the client has no say about their future. Therapy won't be therapy anymore. Insurance companies will be the ones telling therapists what to do with clients because that's where the money comes from. All of our treatment goals will have to meet with insurance approval, even if it doesn't make a difference to the client situation.

"I guess the upshot of all this is that I have great concern about psychotherapy as a field and where it's going, and I don't know what to do about it."

Session 3: Week Three

"Jim, I think that the problem for me is that I have something of an ethical crisis that is almost spiritual in nature. It appears to me that I am being asked to compromise everything that my entire professional career has been based on. I'm not sure I can survive in a system such as this. I just see a deterioration of the practice I loved so much and I anticipate more ineptitude.

"It gets my goat when I think of all those interns who are starting their careers as helping professionals. I see a decline of clinician training and the eventual production of clinical incompetence! An intern in this day and age who has gotten a license probably won't know any more about how to accomplish psychotherapy than the neighborhood alley cat! And with what I was talking about last week, all those new possibilities and new energy and excitement around new psychotherapeutic advancements? Well, it's a damned shame that the low income clients in particular won't have the advantages of those approaches. The only people who will benefit from new psychotherapeutic approaches will be the private pay clients and it will be as it has always been in this country. The best is kept for the rich. Those of us who have to reserve a part of our income base for the insurance trap have to somehow continue to cater to this diagnostic god that's been created whether or not we believe we are doing anything more than creating new barriers to old problems!

"Honestly, Jim, I have great concern about the type of therapists this system will produce in the future. Right now, the licensing boards make sure that all the incoming interns are current with all the theories and right answers to test questions. All the students prepare for the grand-scale standardized test, regurgitate all the right answers and emerge with licenses just because they know how to take a test, not that they have real experience dealing with folks who have serious misfortunes. It takes more to be a qualified therapist than the boards seem to care about. So they know which label to pull out of the hat. I can show them, too, which end of the horse's ass they need to get a grip on but does it mean a thing in the real world? I don't think the people sitting on these boards would recognize a code of ethics to save their lives. They just want to be in compliance with the law, or status quo. Don't quote me on this please, but the future of psychotherapy is, well, in peril.

"For me, there is no way out of this without just getting out of the field all together. I need to get out before I am pushed out for opening my mouth too many times. I have no power the way this whole thing is going and our professional associations have certainly abdicated any responsibility for promoting ethical practice issues at the state and federal levels. I wish I could share with the younger people what it was like once before DSM; what it took to write process recordings until your fingers were blue, develop psycho-social diagnoses that truly focused on client issues, do serious postgraduate study of psychotherapeutic techniques, work with all types of clients with all types of problems. Those were the days when having a degree and a license meant something and the level of integrity of the profession was high. It wasn't about regurgitation of what you have learned so you can pass a test and get a license that means absolutely nothing with this whole new system. Today it is easier to accrue clinical hours to qualify for the licensing exam by working in a public agency doing case-management, than working as an intern in a private practice doing supervised psychotherapy. The rules about office location, percentage of time under supervisory scrutiny and other protocol are much more stringent for private practice than for public agencies, and, frankly, discouraging of that track for interns. Can you imagine being more concerned about the location of where those intern hours are earned, rather than the quality of the experience a person has working with clients? Can you imagine giving your clients a list of test questions to see if they are depressed and then treating them on that basis solely, rather than asking what is happening in their lives?

"The future of psychotherapy has to do more with compliance than effort on the part of the psychotherapist. It has more to do with fitting the right label into the slot than caring about the person who has lost everything and everyone in a hurricane.

"For me, I have to get out of this business before it gets the better of me, Jim. Psychotherapy as a field is something I can't recognize anymore. It's full of protocols, expectations and rules around what label is given and distributed to everyone in town. There isn't room for the psychotherapist who asks about ethics or wants to treat clients as if they can recover from the trauma in their lives. The mentally ill are treated as criminals because they don't fit in anywhere and no one really gets that our mental health system is falling apart. It doesn't matter how much money you throw at something if you can't look at the problem in the face, and that problem is ourselves. My problem is that I am looking the problem in the face, and I don't think I want to work in psychotherapy anymore."

The Ethics of Psychotherapy

Bill's case reveals a myriad of professional dilemmas imposed on him by a national movement in mental health today to require the use of diagnostic labeling as part of clinical practice. What should be examined, however, is the ethical basis for using labeling.

Routinely, graduate schools of today do use ethical guidelines, but the system of diagnostic labeling is relatively new in psychotherapy and thus graduating seniors have not had the chance to evaluate its ethical implications out in the field. Graduate schools in psychology and other counseling based programs are now requiring that students graduate with the basic knowledge of how to diagnose clients using the DSMMD so they will be able to adapt readily to insurance program requirements in medical facilities and mental health or other agencies.

Many students do not receive the same sort of training as Bill did many years ago. Many students today complain about feeling inadequate in the field due to limited clinical experience before getting their licenses. As one recently licensed clinical social worker and drug dependency counselor lamented, "I might as well work at Wal-Mart because this diagnostic stuff is so confusing and it's too much work to keep it all straight. I'm new to this mental health thing and the agencies expect that you have already had training and experience in using it, but I haven't. Now when I get with a client I don't know what to do with it." She continued to describe her experience with receiving a minimal amount of supervised clinical hours devoted to her work in drug prevention counseling where diagnosis and treatment depends on producing quick diagnostic workups to meet agency demands and evaluation of the client's paperwork which she has confirmed may contain up to as many as ten diagnoses per given individual.

Licensure tracks are approved by state boards that determine the number of clinical hours that each intern must have. Supervision of clinical work is required for interns, however constructive supervision may be limited and only provide guidelines to students about how they can meet agency paperwork expectations. The rest of the clinical hours may be superficial in that the intern is often expected to learn through trial and error without assistance about how to interact with clients. This interaction may be specific to looking for the disorder in the client, rather than being tuned in to what is going on in a client's life.

It is important to note that clinical programs do vary, but the focus on specific disorders usually leads the client toward an order for medications instead of practical solutions to basic problems. In other words, "fly by the seat of your pants" clinical skills are often geared toward knowing the protocol for intakes and making symptomatic diagnoses and mental status reports that lead to treatment plans which focus upon the use of medications.

Another common criticism heard from students who were trying to obtain their licenses is that the standardized tests which are used to assess for licensure "mostly measure one's ability to regurgitate material, or to be able to answer abstract test questions that are not useful to anyone working in the field."

What such a deterioration in clinical standards reveals is a primary shift in focus in psychotherapy over the last decade, away from client centered therapy to that of agency centered therapy in which students are becoming experts on picking diagnoses out of the hat. Since there now appears to be over-reliance on diagnostic labeling by governmental entities, insurance companies and social service networks in the area of distribution of human services, students may appear qualified to hang their own shingle right after receiving their licenses. Psychotherapy is now fostering a new flock of psychotherapists that grew up under the DSMMD model. But these newly indoctrinated students reveal a remarkable lack of knowledge about how to work with clients' practical situations without clinging to the diagnostic framework.

It seems that most modern-day treatment approaches lead back to the DSMMD. Any client falling outside of the diagnostic criteria is considered deviant, in some way an enigma to community professionals who can't seem to get their agency protocol together around such issues as dual diagnosis or simple client misfortune. As if this wasn't enough salt in the wound in a field that touted so much revelation during the golden years of psychology and inspired such pioneers as Virginia Satir, Jay Haley, Murray Bowen, Fritz Pearls and Carl Rogers, third party payers are now calling the shots in psychotherapy, as if there was no need for any psychotherapist to reach farther than their current agency mental health status form to discover what to do next.

Finding That Ethical Base

Was there ever an ethical basis for DSMMD? The DSMMD was first published in 1952. A second edition of a hundred-fifty pages was added in

1968. A psychiatrist named Robert Spitzer began his work on a third version in 1974. He took the list of approximately 100 mental diseases recognized by the American Psychiatric Association (A.P.A.), and developed it into an instrument of great popularity and importance, the DSM-III, published in 1980, and its Revision, known as the DSM-III-R, in 1987. The new book grew enormously and captured the imagination of the professional field at the time. It set the tone for the next twenty or so years of the way clients would be viewed and treated by professionals working in every health, medical, mental health or social service entity.

From a scientific perspective, however, there was a glaring flaw from the outset in that there was no official baseline for what constituted normal mental health or behavior, from which accurate assessments of deviant behavior could be determined or studies replicated. Human subjects were chosen for time limited interviews with Spitzer's team of interviewers. As the interviews were conducted, new disorders were added to the growing list of mental disorders. Spitzer's team got together with him on a regular basis to accumulate symptoms and create new disorders, many fabricated in the group sessions themselves. Pathology was in. Finding a disorder, describing it and applying it to anyone who might be affiliated with the interview process was the only thing that mattered.

Even more troubling was the lack of regard for the human subjects. Individuals were interviewed with apparent disregard for personal differences, life struggles, physical or mental limitations, environmental contributors or consideration of one's general plight in life. Symptoms were compiled irrespective of economic stratification, ethnicity, language barriers, employment situations, relationship hardships, family origin, cultural influences, or environmental or systemic barriers. There was no concern among the scientists about whether the data results actually reflected any sort of reality in the subjects' lives.

New disorders thus described were considered reliable by the group, even though critics at the time claimed that the manual lacked a consistent, replicable result and was therefore, also, lacking in scientific validity.

One person who worked closely with Spitzer, and who later was appointed to be the director of development of DSM-IV, is reported to have expressed his concerns about the reliability of Spitzer's results, and reservations about the labeling process. [1]

Public relations efforts after the DSM-III was published convinced the professional community that the reliability of the DSMMD was sound and contributed to its widespread adoption. The DSMMD has only grown in mystique and monetary rewards for the revised versions of the text and related DSMMD materials. No one can dispute the success of the DSMMD. The nation has grown accustomed to the idea that labeling other people is just fine and therefore is reluctant to give it up as an American institution. Labeling other people, after all, fits in with a cultural proclivity and a history filled with discrimination against minority groups.

The question about reliability persists. Studies to test reliability, conducted by the A.P.A. during the development of DSM-IV, yielded results that were similar to those achieved during the '50s and '60s; i.e., showing remarkably little reliability.[2]

The issue of the reliability of the DSMMD raises a serious ethical question. We may not know that the DSMMD is *not* reliable, but neither do we know that it *is* reliable. The question is whether it is ethical, or even legal, to universally apply a diagnostic labeling system that has *not* been proven to be reliable, to human subjects, often without their knowledge or consent! From an ethical standpoint, there also appears to be an amazing lack of attention paid to the life circumstances of human subjects prior to branding them as mentally disordered. If there was anyone concerned about the ethical questions surrounding the issues of labeling, that person was not shouting loud enough during the process of its incorporation into governmental and private medical and mental health insurance programs, legal and court systems, and social service programs over the past twenty-plus years.

Bill's Ethical Considerations

Professional ethics is usually not the topic of conversation among psychotherapists with respect to professional conduct with clients within an agency framework but perhaps such a conversation needs to take place in the agency green room.

No doubt that Bill probably thought about contacting his professional colleagues to find out what their perspectives have been about being employed by New Havens. No doubt his questions have to do with wondering how and why the agency must comply with requirements that control their mental health services. He also probably has a number of questions about the ethics involved with monitoring diagnostic paperwork for insurance purposes.

But not unlike other therapists, Bill is also wondering where the next paycheck will come from. Without the ongoing referrals from the mental health agency Bill might not succeed in his own business. Because of his choice to work with low income clients he needs to be reimbursed by insurance programs for his services. Bill will have to swallow his pride and give in to the party line about making diagnoses in assembly line fashion in order to remain an employee at New Havens. Given the pressures to sustain one's own income, there might very well be the tendency on the part of many therapists (like Bill) to overlook the ethical side of the business and to "not bite the hand that feeds you" even if you would otherwise protest agency protocol. Under an agency's pressure to comply with state and federal guidelines, any therapist might be inclined to ignore his code of ethics to receive his monthly check.

What is inherent in this ethical dilemma is, whether or not Bill should suffer in silence over the loss of his private practice or raise new awareness among community therapists. That is to say, raise the awareness level that such vital members of the psychotherapeutic community are required to participate in unethical practices toward clients, in particular, poor clients. Should he encourage his colleagues to take the ethical position that formalized diagnoses to satisfy agency protocol are unacceptable, and that clients will become more vulnerable to abuse or potential harm from the system?

Whatever Bill concludes, he will never experience the same level of decision making power that he has in his own private practice. In fact, what is lost in the transition from private practice to agency run mental health service is the loss of individual decision making power by the trained therapist and ability to act in the best interest of the client. There will be little flexibility on the part of the agency to allow a therapist to delay or defer diagnosis even when the therapist feels uncertain about a given diagnosis. Any client who receives Medicare or Medicaid insurance is likely to be labeled by Bill with mental illness. This fact should strike a chord of concern in every average consumer of mental health services.

If you are following this line of reasoning, right about now, you may be asking this question: "Where in all this talk about agency protocol are the licensing boards that review professional guidelines?" The state boards purport to protect consumers from abuse or violations of rights in psychotherapy. Apparently they have jumped on the diagnostic labeling bandwagon as well, or at least have been looking the other way instead of reviewing their own code of ethics.

Any therapist who wants to continue to practice in psychotherapy and who expects to be paid from government programs such as Medicare will meet the same fate as Bill. The pressure to eliminate private practices is essentially the result of the government's attempts to change the role of mental health agencies so that they will become accountable for the money invested in mental health services directed at the poor. Serving the poor, downtrodden and misplaced in America has always been the subject of social programs and of course the reason the government needs to control the money invested for this and other social problems. Being accountable is one way to claim that the social problems are being attended to. The system of diagnostic labeling is not, however, a solution to social problems.

Unfortunately, the move toward smoother accountability may mean introducing a new order of social problems not previously anticipated by state and federal agencies. As communities grapple with eligibility requirements for social service programs based on a psychotherapist's diagnosis, the need for new social programs will become more evident to address the growing numbers of mentally disordered clients. The mounting headache of tracking state and federal dollars will inevitably be the responsibility of mental health agencies such as New Havens. Eventually there will be a clamp-down on who is eligible and who is refused support services because of the limited resources and financial backbone.

A new social problem may involve clients becoming overly dependent on social systems to have their basic needs met. Imagine what it will mean to America to have large groups of minorities (homeless, disabled, impoverished, elderly, etc.) standing in line because they are all considered mentally disordered and too disabled to work. Persons who currently qualify for SSI because of a mental disorder are kept from re-entering the work force, even if at some point they might be capable of working a few hours a day. The current system makes deference to whether a person can do some types of work and for few hours. To have SSI means that a person is restricted from working at all; that is to say, toward any sort of self sufficiency, even if there is a drive to acquire life skills that would lead to long term independent living. Individuals like Alma (chapter 1) are viewed as cheaters. Alma was one such person, who wanted to live above abject poverty, but lacked the stamina or physical capabilities to work a full day. These persons continue to be regarded as cheaters in a social system that requires that a person be all disabled or not disabled in order to receive assistance. A psychotherapist may be in the position of providing the right type of diagnosis to ensure SSI, but may also be unaware of the circumstances that could impact the client adversely.

Bill's Ethical Dilemmas

Returning to Bill's situation, Bill wonders how he will retain his professional integrity, treat clients with respect and dignity and remain true to his own code of ethics. There is something of a crisis in the wind for any private practice therapist in Bill's position. Who needs a label and why? In Bill's case, he is wondering why it is that, only the poor, those who are eligible for a type of insurance, are being targeted as mentally disordered. Here it may be important to examine just a few of Bill's ethical dilemmas.

Ethical Dilemma I: To engage in a psychotherapeutic practice based on business practices, rather than putting the best interests of the client first (NASW-CE 1.01) [See Appendix A for National Association of Social Workers Code of Ethics][3]

Bill had been trained in client-centered therapy, valuing the therapeutic alliance as the most salient aspect of the therapeutic process. The psychotherapist of yesteryear was trained in the art of designing a therapeutic program that would serve the client's individualized needs, irrespective of the underlying mental disorder, health condition or life challenges. Those psychotherapists were responsible for their own general conduct and any ethical decisions made in a client's behalf that would be in the best interests of the client. The center of the program was the client, the psychotherapist merely a change agent in the life of the client. The change in approach by today's standards means that Bill will need to change from his traditional client-centered focus to meet the business requirements of insurance programs. Bill recognizes that working under New Havens will present a conflict of interest. New Havens must operate in alignment with other social service entities and insurance programs which means that he will have reduced effectiveness in assisting clients in fighting social system barriers.

Ethical Dilemma II: Bill's challenge is how he can protect the client's privacy and confidentiality (NASW-CE 1.07) or provide adequate informed consent (NASW-CE 1.03) to the sharing of client information in the face of agency requirements for blanket consent, and knowledge that insurance programs have carte blanche to inspect and approve of records for compliance purposes. He must decide how to explain the agency's position to the client: that the client's records may be open to other governmental and social service agencies and medical facilities without client consent in each and every instance.

From the point of view of the consumer, there is no guarantee that privacy and confidentiality will be maintained at any level of service. Most clients routinely sign consent forms for treatment at the start of services, and are only weakly aware that diagnostic labels are being assigned, and records are being kept about the client's progress. The client has no awareness that records are exposed for the purposes of agency accountability. The ethical conclusion for Bill would be that the client has the right to know that confidentiality will not be respected or protected by the client consent form. The client consent form does not protect the client from abuses that can occur as a result of the loss of confidentiality. If Bill were to explain the agency's position to the client and expose the fact that unknown people would be reviewing the client's file, the agency might risk losing clients because the client would be aware of what is at stake. It is unclear if New Havens has considered client confidentiality in the context of agency accountability, or even that the client should be informed of all transactions. Because Bill once had the decision making power to conduct all aspects of private practice, he had the flexibility to make the professional choices that would protect, if not advocate for, his client's best interest. In the new system of diagnostic labeling, clients are not the experts on their own problems nor have the power to make decisions around their level of involvement. A treatment plan that operates in accordance with a diagnosis is all that matters, even if the diagnostic label may potentially harm the client in the future.

Ethical Dilemma III: To participate in the agency's labeling protocol, which encourages mishandling or inappropriate use of labeling that is harmful to clients, or to address the larger systemic problem of social injustice; which is inherent in this type of a system (NASW-CE 6.04).

Not all psychotherapists recognize the signs of social injustice toward individuals on the basis of income, disability, homelessness or, in some cases, age or ethnicity. Many would say that our social service entities are designed to meet the gross needs of these populations. Few would say that they believe that such systems based on diagnostic labeling could have a sinister impact on their client's futures, or, on a large scale, interfere with resolving social problems and in fact discriminate against the poor. Professionals by and large might associate discrimination with the overt civil rights issues of minorities. Not everyone understands the subtleties of class preferential treatment and other insidious forms of institutionalized discrimination. Psychotherapists, because of the professional mask of doing right by clients, may not be so quick to identify that 1) agency procedural guidelines to formalize diagnosis will lead to inappropriate or harmful labels to clients; such persons will be treated differently than those not exposed to the agency protocol; 2) compliance with governmental standards will mean institutionalized discrimination toward the poor because diagnostic labels are given routinely regardless of their accuracy or appropriateness. In other words, everyone will be branded routinely with a harmful label regardless of the reason for seeking therapy or the appropriateness of the label.

Ethical Dilemma IV: Bill's challenge is whether to reduce his own ethical decision making to comply with agency standards, or retain private practice in order to promote the self determination and independence in his clients who are confronting system barriers (NASW-CE 1.02) If Bill works for New Havens he will be significantly restricted in his professional decision making power to protect clients' rights and may be unable to advocate for his clients to remove system barriers.

To illustrate this point, let us take the case example of Mary, who came to Bill as a new client. At the first session, Mary explained to Bill that she really did not need counseling but that she was requesting Bill's services because she needed him to sign off her papers saying she was receiving counseling so she would qualify for HUD housing. Bill was concerned for Mary because the request did not seem based in some life difficulty that Mary was having. Mary explained that she was being required by a social services worker to see a counselor for relapse prevention in order to qualify for HUD. Bill was baffled by Mary's answer and he asked her if she had a drinking problem. Mary responded forthrightly saying, "I had a drinking problem five years ago but I don't anymore. I don't understand why I need relapse prevention because I have no intention of returning to my old lifestyle. Anyhow, they want me to go through counseling so I will be qualified for HUD housing." Bill resented being asked to be something of a watchdog for the government. It was clear that his expertise as a therapist was not being respected and that Mary was being disrespected. What could he do? If he worked for New Havens, he could do nothing because the agency would expect him to comply with the request and Mary would receive a new diagnosis of mental illness that could compromise her in some way. In private practice, he might have the option to advocate, work with the system barriers and perhaps bypass measures that would be more harmful to Mary in the future.

Apart from Bill's dilemma there is a side issue. Mary's rights have been violated by the transmission of diagnostic information to the social service entity without her consent. This is why the requirement for her to receive counseling was made in the first place. Perhaps Mary was unaware that her records were transmitted without her consent; but it is clear that she does not understand that her rights were violated and that social services would have no way of knowing she might have a need for relapse prevention unless records were dispersed among the social agencies.

Furthermore, the assumption that counseling is a safeguard that will keep Mary from returning to drinking assumes that Mary will not exercise her rights to self determination. The assumption is that she cannot be qualified for HUD based on her own statements of her sobriety. Therein lies the rub. Labeling Mary as a substance abuser may in fact have become the hindrance to Mary getting her life on track, demonstrating some self sufficiency which, after all, is the goal, is it not?

The ethics of psychotherapy is only one part of a long, drawn out American saga of dealing with people of cultural, ethnic and economical diversity. Labeling is embedded in American history. The next chapter will help the reader to understand why Americans are infatuated with the need to label.

23

Understanding the Origins of Labeling

Where do we go from here? In order to understand how Americans adopted a system of labeling, it is imperative to examine the roots and philosophical orientation that produced a need of this kind. Knowing some of the historical precursors may help the reader to understand America's preoccupation with labeling.

The origins of labeling can be attributed in part to the phenomenon known as xenophobia, a Greek term referring to the fear of strangers. This fear may be extended to anyone who appears to be different or behaves differently than what is considered characteristic of the norm. Certainly xenophobia is a very primitive, instinctual fear that may have been protective for our distant ancestors. Throughout history, the manifestation of this fear has contributed to the need to label as a way to identify, or cope with, human differences.

Modern day labeling can be traced back to the compilation of English Poor Laws in 1601 which distinguished between the "worthy" and "unworthy" poor, and in other ways institutionalized perceptions of the poor.[1] Under the laws, persons who were designated "worthy" were allowed to beg for alms. Those who were seen as worthy included the disabled who were unable to work, the infirm, the elderly and frail, as well as the "feeble minded" or mentally ill. Able bodied travelers were looked upon by local communities with suspicion and not considered worthy of public assistance. Non-working poor or "ne'er do-wells" were also regarded as unwanted vagrants. They were either run out of town by enforcers of the law or put into prisons and work houses to make their community contributions. When the American Colonies began to put together their own institutions and rules of the law, they adopted the English Poor Laws as their own.[2]

Under this system, the disabled were clearly designated as the beggars of society because they were after all, "unable to work" as defined under law. One backlash from the Poor Laws is very evident today. If a person claims to be disabled and appears to be able to do anything productive, that person may very well be regarded as a "cheater" of the system. Confusion exists over who should qualify for public assistance and who should not, over who is regarded as disabled under the law and who is not. The current eligibility requirements for SSI are a good example, illustrating how eligibility standards are still based on old Poor Law definitions of what constitutes a disability. Persons who apply for SSI will need to prove that they are unable to work and thus disabled under the law before receiving financial assistance and permanent disability status. Naturally, this requires that a diagnosis be made by an appropriate professional that will verify the veracity of the identified person, thus providing the appropriate label in accordance with system demands. Ironically, those persons who already have disabilities, who desire to work and can, experience negative effects or discrimination on the basis of the same old stereotypes about the disabled originating from this early period of American history.

History is full of the experience of identifying people on the basis of xenophobia. People seem to have the need to distinguish "them" from "us," with the underlying message that persons who are different should be regarded with suspicion or fear and that the differences in human attributes warrant this suspicion and fear. The manifestation of xenophobia is certainly justified among warring countries. The concept of "enemy" at times of war re-enforces the notion that the "enemy" is totally reprehensible.

The extension of the need to label, however, can be seen during the unsettled period following the Civil War, which produced many refugees from both sides, variously described as runaways, deserters, or renegades who were regarded with suspicion, and urged to move on, or elsewhere.

The twentieth century was also marked by the Great Depression, during which Americans experienced tremendous hardship, migrating from place to place in order to survive. Descriptive labels began to identify many people as transients, vagrants, hobos, vagabonds or bums. Laws against vagrancy gave rise to the ongoing use of the label, vagrant, as both a descriptive noun and a verb. The term carried with it the connotation that "they" should be avoided, jailed or escorted out of town.

More to the point of this text, in the 1960s America saw the end of the practice of long term custodial care for patients in mental hospitals.

People with apparent mental illness were released to live in the community with the promise of community mental health efforts to provide supportive services. For whatever reason, many of those released did not find permanent homes and formed a population of homeless people who may have been different enough to be seen as mentally ill. The idea of mentally ill persons becoming homeless in communities across America generated the fear that all people who are homeless are mentally ill. An extension of this fear has been the assumption that one must be crazy if one cannot, or does not want, to achieve the "The American Dream." As a result of the emotional hysteria that followed the de-institutionalization, community mental health programs then became the dumping depot for many unresolved social problems that still exist today.

From its inception, America has been based on a system that values democracy, individual justice, equal rights and equal protection under the law. Americans also take pride in education and intellect. So, why is it that American's do not suspend judgment and acknowledge difference without irrational fear?

The answer lies in the ways that labels are used to impose social control. Americans have always had trouble deciding how best to assist its citizens who are less financially or physically capable, perceived as mentally unfit, or who require more attention, money and resources in order to survive the system. Labeling serves the purpose of simplifying, stratifying, and quantifying the distribution of human services, for identifying who is eligible and who is not. Because the use of the DSMMD for labeling serves such a function within the system of provision of mental health services, it has become widely accepted and institutionalized as part of other systems of care.

The human service networks, however, have become increasingly inaccessible to disadvantaged persons because of the heavy emphasis on eligibility standards. Individuals who must confront the barriers of the mental health system are less likely to be able to build their own bridges of access. The label has become a modern tool of segregation. It has re-surfaced as an insidious way of distancing the disadvantaged from the rest of mainstream society. Because more and more impoverished persons are unable to access present service delivery systems, their visibility shines the light on the social problems that the mental health system has failed to fix.

Although many of the homeless have been identified as having serious mental illness, being labeled as homeless carries additional connotations and stigmas. Once labeled homeless, a cultural stereotype is re-enforced in the way these individuals are treated by law enforcement. It becomes seen as necessary to assert some form of social control and compliance because of the belief that transient, homeless people are dangerous. In reality, people who are homeless look like any random number of people of any locale, though many have disabilities in conjunction with poverty and homelessness.

Laws have been created in some states making it a crime to be home-less. Any person identified as homeless brings about immediate suspicion just as it had in the days of the English Poor Laws, post–Civil War era, or Great Depression. The role of law enforcement today is the same: to enforce the laws of the land and to protect the public from lawbreakers. This means enforcing rules and restrictions on anyone who is suspected of sleeping under bridges or of engaging in unwanted panhandling in plain view on city streets.

While most street people do escape notice, many are put into the position of not fitting neatly into any social system due to disability, finan-cial ruin, the inability to work or other personal life tragedies. There has been little effort put into understanding the whole person and the life cir-cumstances that produced the homeless status in the first place. The label of being a homeless person is now synonymous with the term societal out-cast. In some cases, having the label of being homeless does not even mean a person without a home. Take the case of Shelly.

Shelly, a woman who was developmentally challenged, was seen in therapy because she wanted to better her life. She struggled with manag-ing her depression. Most of her life, Shelly had lived with her parents but felt that they had become overbearing because of her cognitive limitations. Shelly wanted to be free to make her own decisions. She decided to move in with her partner and his parent. The three became traveling compan-ions in a small mobile home which had to be moved every few days to avoid the harassment of police. Shelly described an incident to her therapist of what happened when the vehicle had been parked overnight at a local supermarket. A police officer approached the group with baton in hand and told Shelly that "people like you need to leave the area because you are unwanted by everyone and the city should clean homeless scum like you out." Shelly had lived all her life in the general area, as had her trav-eling companions. The group was stunned and did not know how to accom-modate to the policeman's demands that they simply "leave the area." There was no place to go. The mobile home needed repair and was con-stantly breaking down. Shelly had no money to live on aside from her SSI checks each month. Her traveling companions had no money or ability to move away from the area. What options were there for the group?

Apart from the obvious impossibility of the situation for the group, the officer's attitude plainly showed his disdain for people who are gener-ally regarded as homeless. Shelly did not see herself as homeless per se, but there seemed to be no recognition on the part of the officer that the mobile home was in fact the group's home.

This example shows the complexity of the social problems that exist and the cultural attitudes that still prevail regarding individuals who are either labeled or regarded as homeless. What is apparent in Shelly's case is that her problems were not addressed by the police officer. He was simply doing his job by "cleaning the scum" off the street to protect the public. At the same time his answer to the group's problem was to insist that the group become invisible, or "just find homes," as if this opportunity is available to everyone or a matter of personal choice.

Labels serve a greater function for society when they are used as tools of social restraint and segregation, eluding the very essence of the social problem of homelessness. Politicians and legislators can be heard discussing how their laws will keep the streets free from vagrants as if these citizens had none of the same rights as the rest of us. Ironically, the individual who has been labeled homeless may not be able to count on a single diagnosis from a mental health professional for help to access community services because being labeled homeless is a more repugnant societal status. Disabled individuals like Eric illustrate this point.

Eric's Story

Eric had polio during infancy. He wore braces throughout his childhood and was treated somewhat differently by his peers because of his physical disability. Eric did graduate from high school, however, and held down a number of jobs before becoming a chef. He continued this work for many years until post polio syndrome weakened his back and knees to the point where he was no longer able to work in this capacity. Eric lived off of his life savings until it was used up, and it became obvious that he could not afford any housing. Devastated by his lack of income, he applied for SSI and SSDI. He remained in a holding pattern waiting for financial assistance and began his transient lifestyle as a tent camper, making his temporary home in local parks. Every two weeks, he moved to another campground, because park rules disallowed camping for more than two weeks.

Because Eric had Medicaid, he was able to meet with a local doctor who told him that his legs were becoming so weak that he needed surgery. Realizing that he had no home, no place to recover from surgery, Eric grew depressed about his life situation. He began to meet regularly with a therapist after his only dog companion died.

As time went on, it became more difficult for Eric to tent camp and to get around because his legs were too weak. Some months later, he met a woman who was also a tent camper and the two began the process of getting their life back on track. With no money to obtain knee surgery, Eric needed another way to become mobile. He desired to work again but realized there was no way to transport himself anywhere. His partner was able to work and both began to look at housing options again. They tried to find available housing but were unsuccessful. Everything required more money than they had.

Eric became more desperate about his inability to walk and to get around. His therapist encouraged him to seek out a local community agency which specialized in giving away wheelchair equipment to the disabled. Eric sought help from the agency in town but was told because he was homeless and without any possibilities of permanent residence, he was being denied a wheelchair on that basis. Unfortunately, Eric could not use a diagnosis of mental illness to assist him with getting a wheelchair because Eric's therapist believed that his depression was the result of his negative life circumstances and not mental illness.

It is interesting to note that being labeled homeless did not help his situation either. Apparently, Eric did not fit within any system because his particular label happened to be the wrong label. Eric is an example of someone who has fallen through the cracks of both the social service network and the mental health system because neither system possessed a pathway to address Eric's needs.

Recognizing the Cost of the Dream

Americans have historically defined the image of the self-made American. The image of the self-made person has defined what Americans value about their way of life making it even more likely that social problems will be made invisible to the social eye. Americans still believe in the values of rugged individualism, ingenuity, personal accomplishment, affluence and capitalism. Americans also believe that anyone who works hard enough will in time achieve the American Dream. To be able to achieve the dream of affluence and fulfillment, however, a person of difference must make a personal sacrifice and diminish any cultural dissimilarities to acquire the values of the dominant culture. Those persons who do not possess the right qualities of skin color, physical health, economic status, or sexual orientation are offered a different set of conditional civil rights.

Quite frankly, the need to judge another person on the basis of difference is an American trait and part of our puritan history. To assume, however, that the person will or can "disappear" a human difference does not make the difference go away. In Shelly's case, the officer's insistence that she not be impoverished, does not make it so. To insist that the homeless just find homes when they can not afford them does not make it possible.

This American tendency to insist that all people conform to a certain brand of American ideal makes resolving social ills all but impossible. It gets very confusing indeed when Americans use religion and brands of morality to substantiate the reasons why having a difference is unacceptable.

Take for example the issue of gay rights in America. To insist that gays and lesbians in America just not be gay in order to receive benefits and rights given to other members in society, is to deny that there is a difference among people. To insist that individuals simply not be gay will not make it so. Withholding their rights on the basis of difference makes no sense because these Americans will always be there to remind all Americans that they are entitled to the same rights.

To insist that a reading disabled child just become non-disabled because it would be easier for the rest of the class does not make it so. To insist that the child read in the same fashion as other children will not make it so. Acknowledging the child's inability to read through conventional learning might lead to a greater level of problem solving that would serve many children with reading disabilities but this is not considered. Providing audio books instead of removing the child to a resource room to work on reading might solve the problem. The child might be able keep up with same age peers and acquire the same level of knowledge and skills quite naturally. Because of the tendency to treat the disability as if it does not exist, this child is denied the opportunities to learn with peers. Indeed the practice of insisting that this child become non-disabled in order to succeed in school will not make it so.

One can see that in any of the above examples, having a difference matters in America, although the American ideal is that all people are considered equal under the Constitution. Americans can agree that everyone should be able to enjoy the same rights and benefits, providing that individuals avoid calling attention to any difference that might appear aberrant or "non–American." To most Americans the golden rule seems to be, those who do not conform because they cannot will not access the American Dream. Unfortunately, this means that a good number of American citizens are forced out of the system, betrayed by the same system that was designed to protect their differences. Many are forced to rely on some other powerful person or sympathetic system to provide the right kind of label that will help them to access mainstream America again. In some cases this may mean the ability to access the same civil liberties. What stands in the way of equality for all American citizens is the perpetual need to judge or label other people on the basis of differences. There seems to be, however, the need to cling to the old puritan ethic, i.e., if the worst happens to people, they had a hand in their own decline not that our inability to solve social problems often lies at the heart of human tragedy.

The ultimate myth is that social problems are solved by systems of care, institutions that are designed to take care of all the scary people with problems not understood. The hope is that the problems will diminish in time or become invisible, and not become the social responsibility of us all. With the removal of social responsibility, many people can live their personal reality believing that it is not their responsibility to invest in the lives of individuals less fortunate.

If Americans want to deal with the failures of the present mental health system, it is important that it be recognized that plenty of money and profit has been made from human suffering and that Americans are not better off because of it. Most Americans, at one time or another, will experience the need for financial assistance. Americans are already sounding the call for better medical care and access to cheaper medications. The baby boomers of today will need someone to pay for caregivers, as retirement without savings or Social Security becomes commonplace. Sooner or later Americans will have to succumb to the hardships of living in a perfect society where no one receives anything without being worthy of the handout.

A Change in Orientation

The only way to avoid the myths is to get out of the dilemma of using devastating DSMMD diagnostic labels, and to change the very nature and essence of the provision of mental health services in this country. The strongest ethical argument against using labeling is that it involves subjective judgment on the part of the professional. For psychotherapists who use labeling, it is largely a presumption of human behavior, not a truth for the individual because it is not an accurate assessment of an individual's life experiences.

A diagnosis has limited longevity with questionable utility beyond the immediate scope of therapy. Without a focus on how the client functions within the life situation, it is doubtful that the client will be able to generalize learned skills when confronted with a new life paradigm.

There is an interesting dynamic that evolves over time with individuals who have received many diagnoses over the years. The labels actually begin to obscure the functional abilities or limitations of the person, making it impossible for other service providers to know where to begin with certain clients. It may be clear to a service provider who encounters a particular client that the person's behaviors suggest mental illness. But there may still be a fuzzy sense of non-clarity about the exact nature and origin of the individual's difficulties, especially when the diagnosis has changed numerous times on paper, with the exchange of hands of differing professionals. In fact, there is often a complete lack of communication about how the client functions on a practical level. The diagnostic report becomes an inadequate tool because of the apparent lack of professional attention to the client's function.

Take the case scenario below of Mr. Wong, a vocational counselor who takes on a client with obvious mental illness. His own requirement as a vocational counselor is to provide the client with vocational training which might lead to a job in the future to sustain the client's long term independence. This is how Mr. Wong described the problem:

Mr. Wong sat across from his client and wondered which one of the eleven diagnoses of mental illness stated in the diagnostic report was true about the client. All the diagnoses were different and grew progressively more serious over the course of the client's life. The client was now sitting in the room across from Mr. Wong. He was not moving in his chair, silent with the exception of grating his teeth nervously and staring down at his hands, not making eye contact with Mr. Wong. It was Mr. Wong's role as a vocational rehabilitation counselor to find a vocational avenue for this client. He wondered where he should begin. It was obvious from the report that he was diagnosed with mental illness because of his bizarre behaviors and avoidance of social contact with other people. As Mr. Wong continued to read the report he gleaned little information from what was provided. What could he do, other than have his client re-evaluated again, which might not give him any more useful information than was in the report?

The change from using the DSMMD as the primary assessment method and main source for treatment direction means the choice to adopt a more pragmatic, functional approach. Mr. Wong and other service providers would benefit by having descriptive analyses of client function. It makes intervention possible and the range of services more meaningful to the goals of each client.

Avoiding the reliance on labeling means looking instead to the way people address, acknowledge, adapt to, or accommodate to their immediate environments. In other words, embracing a more dimensional view of human behavior rather than ignoring the various aspects of life challenges that influence behavior.

With a focus geared toward functionality, there would be an obvious change in the role of the psychotherapist to the client. The role of the psychotherapist should be directed toward a focus on the functional life challenges of the client. This may include but is not limited to the emotional impact of life challenges. The DSMMD has brought a focus to therapy which has been primarily based on the client's symptoms and emotional state. The functional approach to working with clients means moving away from the notion that all behavior must be viewed as residual of a mental disorder.[3]

The move toward viewing clients as functional beings rather than their mental disease means recognizing that clients are impacted by a myriad of significant influences: internal, social and environmental.

Internal contributors include the ways the client manifests personality traits, self concept and self esteem, unique physiology, temperament, ability to regulate mood swings, how life experiences are interpreted and in more general terms how the client is equipped to think, respond and remember. Social influences might include the ways the client is shaped by important social relationships, he adapts to social rules or internalizes social standards. Environmental influences might include life events such as the loss of a job, acquiring a disability, or the death of a loved one. These influences carry different weight for every person, affecting their abilities to deal with real life challenges. Assisting a person to function more effectively must involve acknowledging the ways an individual operates in the here and now, recognizing that the person has been shaped by a combination of these influences.

To work toward increasing a client's function is to move the relationship of provider to consumer, psychotherapist to client, into a more equitable and trust-based relationship.

If there is a more equitable relationship, clients become more equal participants in the process of developing a working plan to measure progress toward achievable goals and be motivated to move toward any assistive process they need to involve themselves with. Perhaps the nature of the interactive relationship between psychotherapist and clients would become more of a contractual behavioral agreement for what is obtainable, which is more aligned with the concept of a business relationship, that of fee for service. To create a system in which labeling is eliminated as the legal tender for payment for psychotherapy would mean consumers could have the confidence that they could benefit from psychotherapy without having to share their personal, confidential information with huge corporate entities.

The therapeutic alliance would mean the agreement to work toward a mutual goal that would assist the client with getting what is needed in order to deal with real life challenges. Not relying on a label to define a client would leave the door open for the client to define the problem. The psychotherapist could then arrive at an agreement with the client to work on a mutually satisfactory goal of achievement which could be measured over time. By using the client's definition of the problem, the psychotherapist would see that there is an increase in the client's investment in the therapeutic process because the client feels included in the outcome.

Accomplishment would be used as the unit of measurement that determines progress.

The psychotherapist in this instance is more of a facilitator and educator, assisting clients to become more astute about their own behavioral repertoire, discussing the realm of possibilities for behavioral change that will enable the clients to become more effective at solving problems and generalizing these skills to other life areas. Clients who are freed from being labeled will naturally learn to trust their own abilities, tune into strengths and be motivated to achieve results rather than setting out to fulfill a treatment plan of a psychotherapist whose agenda is to "cure" the "unhealthy mind" (which is an unobtainable goal). If clients are freed from the effects of labeling by others they are freed from being viewed as pathological.

Clients who believe in an intact self will experience tighter connections between themselves and larger social systems, experience more fulfillment in human relationships, be capable of removing system barriers within their immediate social environments and react as effectual beings within other social contexts such as employment or school settings.

Before change in the present day system can occur with some facility, a change in philosophical orientation toward viewing clients from a functional standpoint by psychotherapists needs to be employed. This means suspending the notion that all behavior that a client manifests is residual of mental instability or of a particular disorder. It means suspending the notion that the DSMMD is the only way to arrive at a complete understanding of the individual. It also would mean suspending the notion that the DSMMD provides the only worthwhile information relevant to assessment and treatment and that diagnostic labeling leads to addressing the real problems a client has.

It has already been suggested that the DSMMD continues to be the desirable manual to identify and diagnose serious mental illness. It must, however, be the responsibility of the therapeutic community and licensure boards to draw boundaries around its application and use within the social service and community based contexts. Much of the communication between governmental and community entities has relied heavily upon the DSMMD labeling system. The drive should be to get the DSMMD out of being the hub of distribution of human services.

24

Defining What We Mean by Serious Mental Illness

Most mental health providers will argue that they are competent to use the DSMMD when they start practicing with their licenses. There is an assumption that the practicing therapist automatically has earned the right to own the role of diagnostician, to use diagnostic labeling involving all cases and to define mental illness in all cases. But, can it or should it be found in every person? By what degree does a person fit with the label of serious mental illness?

Erving Goffman[1] and Thomas Szasz[2] have raised the issue of whether mental illness exists at all, and both have referred to it as a myth. Do we need to label every person as having some form of mental illness for the purpose of professional usage, or should mental illness be defined according to cultural context?

The authors wanted to obtain information about how mental illness is viewed and treated in the countries of Denmark, Canada, and New Zealand. Contact was made with a psychologist in Denmark who was willing to consult with the authors about Denmark's system and view of mental health services.[3]

According to the information obtained, Denmark's approach is not based on diagnostic labeling. The DSMMD is not used. The International Classification of Diseases, Tenth Revision (ICD-10) is used between professionals to discuss a client's condition or level of function. When asked if there is ever a label given for serious mental illness, this source answered that labels are not generally used. Not even the number system to communicate between professionals is used as a general practice. When a serious diagnosis is made such as schizophrenia, it is considered a diagnosis of last resort. The diagnosis is not made by a single mental health diagnostician but by a board of professionals which makes numerous evaluations over time to arrive at the definitive diagnosis.

Notice the sharp contrast between the tendency not to label in Denmark as compared to the rapid and often punitive way in which diagnostic labeling is employed in the U.S. The change toward a more positive approach toward mental illness would mean perhaps adopting an approach similar to Denmark's in which a number system could be utilized in place of labeling but then is restricted in its broad usage. The other point made is that the professionals collaborate to arrive at a diagnosis of severe mental illness. Up until the diagnosis is made the client is freed from the negative stigma and consequences resulting from labeling.

In the search to understand how other mental health systems operate, Denmark, Canada and New Zealand shared some commonality. In sharp contrast to the U.S., the mental health systems of these countries are considered to be a part of the national public health program paid for by the government. Not all of the services rendered are paid for by the government, nor all medications. The emphasis, however, seems to be based in a holistic health approach in which the "whole of the person" is served in a clinical fashion, meaning that all citizens will receive at least minimal medical if not mental health services. The cost to the client, if there is one, is minimal. The public health systems determine the level of services based on severity of the problem.

Another commonality seems to be that all persons may be assigned a general physician for primary care, who then determines how severe the mental health problem is. It is the responsibility of the general physician to refer the client on to specialists in mental health. These could be psychologists, or psychiatrists who provide ongoing mental health services.

In Denmark, the government pays for ten visits for problems of persons with personal crises (such as death of a loved one, or rape). After the ten visits the client has the option to continue therapy but pays for the rest of the visits. The person always has the choice to contact a psychotherapist independently but the understanding is that the individual would pay for such services.

In the event that the general doctor feels that the client has less troubling problems but chooses to see a therapist, the client might end up paying for psychotherapy. Clients usually pay into the system for medications. Clients who feel that they cannot pay for all the services can purchase health insurance which prolongs payments.

In Canada, individuals can use the public health system to access general physicians who will refer clients to psychotherapists. Six therapy sessions are paid for by Canada's government. If an individual feels the need to pursue ongoing therapy beyond the six visits, that person incurs the costs.[4]

New Zealand has a similar system in which the clients must first be seen by a general doctor through the public health system who then refers the person on for intensive psychotherapy if the doctor determines that the severity of the client's problem warrants further attention from the specialists in mental health.[5]

The idea behind having a public health system in which the government pays for services directly to cover the physical and psychological conditions is controversial in the U.S. primarily because of the age old question of how much government should be involved in the lives of its citizens. Given how many people in the U.S. are not served under health care programs or health insurance plans, perhaps it is time to take another look at the provision of services in this country. Other old disputes involve how much control should states have over their own economies and social programs. What should be the role of private enterprise regarding the current health care system?

One positive aspect of having a strong government involvement with a health care system is that generally there is more of an invested concern on the part of taxpayers for existing social service programs they support, making sure that the outcome of governmental supports benefit citizens directly. With strong government involvement, more citizens are likely to be covered. The criticisms are likely to be that some services would only weakly address the needs of most people, that the programs might not adequately address more serious health problems in an expedient fashion (which is Denmark's problem), and with high numbers of people using services, there is a likelihood that over time the overall programs might dwindle in size with a continuously diminishing financial base. This might lead to a prioritization of who gets served first, for what problems, in order of severity.

There is one additional advantage of the Danish system according to our source. Because of an increase in governmental involvement, Danish citizens can expect that if they acquire disabilities, they will receive immediate financial support. Comparatively, individuals in the U.S who acquire disabilities can expect to wait for any federal financial assistance or confirmation of SSI for a minimum of two to three years. On top of the life challenges that the individual encounters because of a new disability, individuals are faced with experiencing an inhospitable application process for disability payments, continual rejection of their applications and having the unnecessary burden of providing paper proof that they are worthy of receiving financial support as a full fledged disabled person who cannot work.

In short, the average person can expect to experience added frustration and hardship as the result of being in a nebulous holding pattern because of lack of financial supports. One only has to turn on the television set to see veterans dismayed and disillusioned with the government over the delay of services and withholding of financial supports they thought that they would receive immediately in order to get their lives back on track again.

In America, the lack of government involvement and inaccessibility can lead to more catastrophic social problems for those who lose their jobs due to disabilities. Not only do individuals lose their way of life, they may use up their life savings waiting for a more permanent disability status. Some may lose their homes and become homeless. The meager state disability checks which clients might apply for do not begin to assist a client with transitioning into a more restrictive lifestyle based on less functionality.

It could be that Americans still have a view that the American health care and mental health systems are the best there are. No one will dispute the advancement in science or medicine, however, it may take longer for Americans to realize that fewer citizens are reaping the benefits that are afforded to the wealthy and that the rest of the world may be looking on wondering "how could this be?" At one point in the conversation, the Danish psychologist was asked for her opinion. "What do people in your country think about the American health care or mental health system?" She answered this way: "I think they feel that the American system is unjust. America has the best doctors in the world, but only people with money can benefit."

About Serious Mental Illness

The authors wanted to know more about who provides mental health services in Denmark, how serious mental illness is dealt with in that country, the role of the professional and range of services to offer a new perspective to Americans.

When asked who can provide mental health services in Denmark several key points were discussed. First, all doctors, nurses, health service providers and social workers have training or educational background in mental health. They often provide mental health services within the context of their respective jobs. These professionals have no special degrees, certifications or licenses, however the professionals must complete education which includes hours for practical application and testing for each area of specialization. The tests are designed to meet the criteria of the job or the site in which the professional works. A psychologist completes an educational program lasting usually six and one-half years.

With regards to the severely mentally ill, formal diagnosis is done in a hospital by psychiatrists and as stated above, the diagnosis is reached by group decision. Before a diagnosis is made however, terms like "lapses" or "episodes" are used to describe the condition in place of more debilitating judgments. In the case of very serious conditions such as schizophrenia, doctors are very reluctant to come to that conclusion or diagnosis because it has ongoing negative consequences within the system for the individual. For individuals who have been diagnosed, treatment is started in the person's home if that is possible. The individual is expected to come to the hospital for meetings and a daily program.

In Denmark, the level of involvement remains high with the client, maintained on a daily basis with clients after a diagnosis is reached. The client is required to participate in programs based at home first. In America, these clients diagnosed with mental illness might benefit from this approach as a least restrictive environment to learn more functional ways of dealing with the mental disability. With those persons having no home, the challenge might be to have transitional housing to begin with and then provide the bridges to more permanent dwellings.

According to the Danish psychologist, treatment may need to be started in the hospital where the client may be evaluated in terms of how well they function and assessed for the range of lifestyle possibilities they might have. During the time the person is in the hospital, a variety of medicines is given to find a balance in the individual's system. As soon as is feasible, the person is moved to a group home with other persons having severe diagnoses as well. A social worker is assigned to visit the individual and assist with teaching living skills and taking personal care of themselves. Some of these individuals will spend their entire lives in group homes because they are unable to move toward self sufficiency or independent living in an apartment for example. If the person is able to move out of the group home, the social worker helps with the move and keeps in touch with the person regularly during the adjustment period. The adjustment period could take a long time. The government pays for the entire process. The disabled individual receives a pension from the government, which pays the rent and living expense.

The reader may be prone to ask at this juncture, where do we go from here? The American mental health system is in crisis. People are falling through the cracks of an inept and heartless approach to solving social problems. What change needs to take place that would be more responsive to the needs of disenfranchised citizens?

25

Facing the Ultimate Challenge

Coming to Terms with the American Approach to the Provision of Mental Health Services

In order to consider what changes need to be made to the American approach to the provision of mental health services, there needs to be a basic understanding of it. What is the American mental health system? How is it composed and what are the goals of this American ideal?

The concepts of pathology and mental health prevention have captured the essence of the field of mental health. Professionals in the field have been preoccupied with the idea that mental health can be determined by identifying and classifying its opposite, pathology. There is a public consensus that mental instability needs correction. There is also unspoken collective understanding that citizens who are mentally healthy need to be protected from those defined as unhealthy in our society, even though the elusive and often subjective understanding of normal mental health has never been clearly defined by professionals in the field.

Nevertheless, the idea has caught on over time that the ultimate goal should be to move toward mental health, and that mental illness should be eradicated whenever, wherever it is found. Within that context, it has become the responsibility of the American mental health system to maintain a basic standard of mental health by implementing programs which will prevent the onset of mental illness, and provide the most comprehensive approaches for its treatment.

Structural Considerations

The American mental health system is composed of a coordinated network of mental health facilities which are designed to provide a range of mental health services within every state and county across the nation. Mental health facilities, although funded and supported by governmental entities, are primarily controlled and run by state and local governments. Facilities are either public facilities or privately owned facilities such as some hospitals, clinics and most psychiatric hospitals. Privately owned facilities may operate in conjunction with public programs and share services in a particular locale depending upon the availability of community resources and type of persons served.[1]

It is interesting to note that over time, general hospitals have taken more of an active role in the emergency response to the needs of the severely mentally ill who enter and exit local systems of care. Institutional psychiatric placements are no longer the primary entrance and exit houses for the mentally ill. Civil right laws have come to liberate the mentally ill from overcommitment to these facilities, causing a new type of social problem to arise, that of how to provide ongoing care to a population that transitions in and out of systems of care and independent living. At the community level, intervention involves decisions that need to be made based on available resources for existing services. Communities do receive funds to provide after care and case management for the coordination of services to the mentally ill, but the extent of services rendered do not meet the ongoing needs of this population.

With regards to persons considered transient, controversy is generated in communities about how to accommodate the large numbers of homeless people, how services should be provided, if at all, because of the confusion over who qualifies as simply homeless, or who is mentally ill. There appears to be less confusion when the person is both homeless and mentally ill. As has been already stated, transient individuals may not be mentally ill, but have other disabilities or compounding problems. In some communities, confusion arises to an all new high when individuals have to qualify for receiving shelter by being required to have had a past of using drugs. In other words, some of the homeless are turned away from homeless centers based on not qualifying as a past drug user. Given where the money trail ends, the federal money that has been designated for drug prevention and substance abuse programs may account for the confusing eligibility requirements. Perhaps the confusion would not exist if the stereotypes about the homeless did not exist!

Following the Money Trail

One can follow the money trail by studying the hierarchy of administration at the federal, state and local levels. At the top level the Substance

Abuse and Mental Health Services Administration operates under the federal Department of Health and Human Services.[2] Through this entity federal block grants are created, then sent to the states to implement statewide and countywide programs.

Professional associations operating at the federal, state and local levels also participate in the implementation of mental health facilities. Other influential voluntary associations participate as well, such as the National Mental Health Association and consumer based organizations such as the National Alliance of the Mentally Ill.

The National Institute of Mental Health oversees the community support programs. In addition, there are specific departments of the government such as the Department of Veterans Affairs which oversees the mental health services and psychiatric care of veterans. Other mental health programs are also financially supported through the Office of Rehabilitation and by the Department of Defense. Using the money from the federal block grants, state mental health departments, as well as state health departments control the operations of mental health services across each state. Some community mental health services may be supported financially through the state departments of education, money funded through designated special education programs.

Funding can be awarded through grants from the Community Support program to pay for specific programs and coordination of services for the mentally ill. This entity also provides money for state and local demonstration projects designed to target special populations, for example, children with special needs.

At the local levels, it is easy to see how health insurance programs have grown in power and influence over the years, paying for some mental health services and gradually playing a larger role in deciding who receives psychotherapy. The restrictions on coverage have encouraged psychotherapists to utilize more severe diagnoses so that services will be paid. Medicaid and Medicare, however, continue to provide financial support for psychiatric services but eligibility standards are restrictive.

Federal money can be also accessed by the states for particular programs. Each state must first develop a comprehensive community service plan that will address the needs of children or adults before funds may be approved at the federal level.

Mental health programs at the local levels usually receive their share of money from that received at the state level. Community mental health programs generally consist of services which include: diagnosis, treatment, care within hospitals or other community based programs, emergency care, case management, therapy and professional assistance with treatment, and educational services.

Trying to follow the money trail and account for services to consumers is like trying to unscramble eggs. Suffice it to say that of the amount of money that is appropriated at the federal level, the administration of that money at the federal, state and county levels reduces the amount left for services to consumers to a fraction of that appropriated.

The Grand New Deal

If the authors were to propose a new way for services to be funded and provided, it would start with the federal block grants that are sent to the states. The following steps might ensure that every client is served and receives the benefits of mental health services without the negative impact of diagnostic labeling.

1. Universal health coverage should be provided for every citizen in America regardless of whether the person is a taxpayer or not. The health care system would not only provide medical services, but also include mental health services.
2. Taxes would be paid into the system as they are now. Taxpayers would have a percentage of their taxes put to one side to pay for universal health care in their state. Thus, the taxpayers would be served locally by the money they directly provided. The money would be set aside at the state level and held in a pool for citizens.
3. Money received from the federal government in the form of block grants for mental health services would also be held at the state level in the money pool for mental health services. States can also apply to the federal Community Support Program for money to provide an additional pool for indigent people who have traditionally been cut off from health care programs that support mental health services.

What This Means to You

1. Medical providers would be asked to meet with each person who desires counseling or to work with a psychotherapist, any client who has a mental health need. The medical provider would be paid through the same state mental health money pool to serve the client at this initial stage. The provider would be reimbursed after sending in the application to the state for services rendered with the person's name and reason for the visit.
2. If the medical provider and the person agree that the problem

requires psychotherapy, the provider would refer the client on to a private therapist in the community.

3. To access payment for mental health services, the psychotherapist would submit an application form to the state pool for payment, indicating the name of the client and level of need for services.

4. If the need requires psychotherapy beyond ten sessions, the individual would agree to pay privately for additional psychotherapy. If the individual is unable to pay the total cost, the psychotherapist and client could apply directly to the federal pool for money to be paid for additional services.

5. When psychotherapy services are terminated, the records would be given to the individual. Records at the state level would be destroyed when the psychotherapist is paid for the last time. The client would have the option of sharing the report or record with a psychotherapist or service provider in the community if applying for services that require that information. Social service entities would have to rely on other information about the client to substantiate services.

6. Clients who have more involved mental illness would be referred on to a board made up of five or six local professionals, appointed and paid for by the state, who are trained, specialize and are certified by licensure boards in diagnosing severe mental illness.

7. The board would operate out of local centers or a Community Based Center for the Integration of Persons with Mental Illness. These CBCs would receive the money that has been directed in the past for public mental health facilities. The money would be used to set up programs and housing to support those persons with severe mental illness. The center could also be the service gateway for persons walking in off the street and need an entry into a social service, medical care or mental health program. A coordinator would help these persons access the appropriate services.

8. If a determination is made by the board that a person has severe mental illness, several assessments would be made to determine the client's level of functioning, need for and tolerance of medication, ability to live independently, or need for training in life skills.

9. Clients who are diagnosed with severe mental illness would be placed in integrated settings from least restrictive to most restrictive placement options depending on level of functionality. Much like Denmark, social workers and other medical care providers might have a hand in the education and training in life skills of clients but the focus would be on learning skills for living life inde-

pendently, contributing to integrated work settings in the community and financial self sufficiency. Self determination and civil rights of the mentally ill would be respected as these individuals would fully participate in the evolvement of their own programs to the extent they are able. Programs might be developed to engage these individuals in job related contexts that pertain to their levels of functionality.

Afterthoughts

In order for every American to benefit from the ideals of equality for all, there needs to be the recognition that not all the civil rights are enjoyed by all the people. Diagnostic labeling is just one more device in our society that has been used to divide people and represents a new variety of institutionalized discrimination. Labeling does, in effect, segregate disadvantaged persons from the mainstream of American life.

The American Dream has always been held up as a one-way road to success, but has never been accessible to everyone. Refocusing the American Dream toward the humanitarian approach of inclusion is perhaps a more worthy pursuit.

Appendix: Code of Ethics of the National Association of Social Workers

Approved by the 1996 NASW Delegate Assembly
Revised by the 1999 NASW Delegate Assembly

Preamble

The primary mission of the social work profession is to enhance human well-being and help meet the basic human needs of all people, with particular attention to the needs and empowerment of people who are vulnerable, oppressed, and living in poverty. A historic and defining feature of social work is the profession's focus on individual well-being in a social context and the well-being of society. Fundamental to social work is attention to the environmental forces that create, contribute to, and address problems in living.

Social workers promote social justice and social change with and on behalf of clients. "Clients" is used inclusively to refer to individuals, families, groups, organizations, and communities. Social workers are sensitive to cultural and ethnic diversity and strive to end discrimination, oppression, poverty, and other forms of social injustice. These activities may be in the form of direct practice, community organizing, supervision, consultation, administration, advocacy, social and political action, policy development and implementation, education, and research and evaluation. Social workers seek to enhance the capacity of people to address their own needs. Social workers also seek to promote the responsiveness of organizations, communities, and other social institutions to individuals' needs and social problems.

The mission of the social work profession is rooted in a set of core values. These core values, embraced by social workers throughout the profession's history, are the foundation of social work's unique purpose and perspective:

- service
- social justice
- dignity and worth of the person
- importance of human relationships
- integrity
- competence.

This constellation of core values reflects what is unique to the social work profession. Core values, and the principles that flow from them, must be balanced within the context and complexity of the human experience.

Purpose of the NASW Code of Ethics

Professional ethics are at the core of social work. The profession has an obligation to articulate its basic values, ethical principles, and ethical standards. The NASW Code of Ethics sets forth these values, principles, and standards to guide social workers' conduct. The Code is relevant to all social workers and social work students, regardless of their professional functions, the settings in which they work, or the populations they serve.

The NASW Code of Ethics serves six purposes:

1. The Code identifies core values on which social work's mission is based.
2. The Code summarizes broad ethical principles that reflect the profession's core values and establishes a set of specific ethical standards that should be used to guide social work practice.
3. The Code is designed to help social workers identify relevant considerations when professional obligations conflict or ethical uncertainties arise.
4. The Code provides ethical standards to which the general public can hold the social work profession accountable.
5. The Code socializes practitioners new to the field to social work's mission, values, ethical principles, and ethical standards.
6. The Code articulates standards that the social work profession itself can use to assess whether social workers have engaged in

unethical conduct. NASW has formal procedures to adjudicate ethics complaints filed against its members.* In subscribing to this Code, social workers are required to cooperate in its implementation, participate in NASW adjudication proceedings, and abide by any NASW disciplinary rulings or sanctions based on it.

*For information on NASW adjudication procedures, see NASW Procedures for the Adjudication of Grievances.

The Code offers a set of values, principles, and standards to guide decision making and conduct when ethical issues arise. It does not provide a set of rules that prescribe how social workers should act in all situations. Specific applications of the Code must take into account the context in which it is being considered and the possibility of conflicts among the Code's values, principles, and standards. Ethical responsibilities flow from all human relationships, from the personal and familial to the social and professional.

Further, the NASW Code of Ethics does not specify which values, principles, and standards are most important and ought to outweigh others in instances when they conflict. Reasonable differences of opinion can and do exist among social workers with respect to the ways in which values, ethical principles, and ethical standards should be rank ordered when they conflict. Ethical decision making in a given situation must apply the informed judgment of the individual social worker and should also consider how the issues would be judged in a peer review process where the ethical standards of the profession would be applied.

Ethical decision making is a process. There are many instances in social work where simple answers are not available to resolve complex ethical issues. Social workers should take into consideration all the values, principles, and standards in this Code that are relevant to any situation in which ethical judgment is warranted. Social workers' decisions and actions should be consistent with the spirit as well as the letter of this Code.

In addition to this Code, there are many other sources of information about ethical thinking that may be useful. Social workers should consider ethical theory and principles generally, social work theory and research, laws, regulations, agency policies, and other relevant codes of ethics, recognizing that among codes of ethics social workers should consider the NASW Code of Ethics as their primary source. Social workers also should be aware of the impact on ethical decision making of their clients' and their own personal values and cultural and religious beliefs and practices. They should be aware of any conflicts between personal and professional values and deal with them responsibly. For additional guidance social workers should consult the relevant literature on professional ethics and ethical decision making and seek appropriate consultation when faced with ethical dilemmas. This may involve consultation with an agency-based or social work organization's ethics committee, a regulatory body, knowledgeable colleagues, supervisors, or legal counsel.

Instances may arise when social workers' ethical obligations conflict with agency policies or relevant laws or regulations. When such conflicts occur, social workers must make a responsible effort to resolve the conflict in a manner that is consistent with the values, principles, and standards expressed in this Code. If a reasonable resolution of the conflict does not appear possible, social workers should seek proper consultation before making a decision.

The NASW Code of Ethics is to be used by NASW and by individuals, agencies, organizations, and bodies (such as licensing and regulatory boards, professional liability insurance providers, courts of law, agency boards of directors, government agencies, and other professional groups) that choose to adopt it or use it as a frame of reference. Violation of standards in this Code does not automatically imply legal liability or violation of the law. Such determination can only be made in the context of legal and judicial proceedings. Alleged violations of the Code would be subject to a peer review process. Such processes are generally separate from legal or administrative procedures and insulated from legal review or proceedings to allow the profession to counsel and discipline its own members.

A code of ethics cannot guarantee ethical behavior. Moreover, a code of ethics cannot resolve all ethical issues or disputes or capture the richness and complexity involved in striving to make responsible choices within a moral community. Rather, a code of ethics sets forth values, ethical principles, and ethical standards to which professionals aspire and by which their actions can be judged. Social workers' ethical behavior should result from their personal commitment to engage in ethical practice. The NASW Code of Ethics reflects the commitment of all social workers to uphold the profession's values and to act ethically. Principles and standards must be applied by individuals of good character who discern moral questions and, in good faith, seek to make reliable ethical judgments.

Ethical Principles

The following broad ethical principles are based on social work's core values of service, social justice, dignity and worth of the person, importance of human relationships, integrity, and competence. These principles set forth ideals to which all social workers should aspire.

Value: Service

Ethical Principle: Social workers' primary goal is to help people in need and to address social problems.

Social workers elevate service to others above self-interest. Social workers draw on their knowledge, values, and skills to help people in need and to address social problems. Social workers are encouraged to volunteer some portion of their professional skills with no expectation of significant financial return (pro bono service).

Value: Social Justice

Ethical Principle: Social workers challenge social injustice.

Social workers pursue social change, particularly with and on behalf of vulnerable and oppressed individuals and groups of people. Social workers' social change efforts are focused primarily on issues of poverty, unemployment, discrimination, and other forms of social injustice. These activities seek to promote sensitivity to and knowledge about oppression and cultural and ethnic diversity. Social workers strive to ensure access to needed information, services, and resources; equality of opportunity; and meaningful participation in decision making for all people.

Value: Dignity and Worth of the Person

Ethical Principle: Social workers respect the inherent dignity and worth of the person.

Social workers treat each person in a caring and respectful fashion, mindful of individual differences and cultural and ethnic diversity. Social workers promote clients' socially responsible self-determination. Social workers seek to enhance clients' capacity and opportunity to change and to address their own needs. Social workers are cognizant of their dual responsibility to clients and to the broader society. They seek to resolve conflicts between clients' interests and the broader society's interests in a socially responsible manner consistent with the values, ethical principles, and ethical standards of the profession.

Value: Importance of Human Relationships

Ethical Principle: Social workers recognize the central importance of human relationships.

Social workers understand that relationships between and among people are an important vehicle for change. Social workers engage people as partners in the helping process. Social workers seek to strengthen relationships among people in a purposeful effort to promote, restore, maintain, and enhance the well-being of individuals, families, social groups, organizations, and communities.

Value: Integrity

Ethical Principle: Social workers behave in a trustworthy manner.

Social workers are continually aware of the profession's mission, values, ethical principles, and ethical standards and practice in a manner consistent with them. Social workers act honestly and responsibly and promote ethical practices on the part of the organizations with which they are affiliated.

Value: Competence

Ethical Principle: Social workers practice within their areas of competence and develop and enhance their professional expertise.

Social workers continually strive to increase their professional knowledge and skills and to apply them in practice. Social workers should aspire to contribute to the knowledge base of the profession.

Ethical Standards

The following ethical standards are relevant to the professional activities of all social workers. These standards concern (1) social workers' ethical responsibilities to clients, (2) social workers' ethical responsibilities to colleagues, (3) social workers' ethical responsibilities in practice settings, (4) social workers' ethical responsibilities as professionals, (5) social workers' ethical responsibilities to the social work profession, and (6) social workers' ethical responsibilities to the broader society.

Some of the standards that follow are enforceable guidelines for professional conduct, and some are aspirational. The extent to which each standard is enforceable is a matter of professional judgment to be exercised by those responsible for reviewing alleged violations of ethical standards.

1. Social Workers' Ethical Responsibilities to Clients
1.01 Commitment to Clients

Social workers' primary responsibility is to promote the well-being of clients. In general, clients' interests are primary. However, social workers' responsibility to the larger society or specific legal obligations may on limited occasions supersede the loyalty owed clients, and clients should be so advised. (Examples include when a social worker is required by law to report that a client has abused a child or has threatened to harm self or others.)

1.02 Self-Determination

Social workers respect and promote the right of clients to self-determination and assist clients in their efforts to identify and clarify their goals. Social workers may limit clients' right to self-determination when, in the social workers' professional judgment, clients' actions or potential actions pose a serious, foreseeable, and imminent risk to themselves or others.

1.03 Informed Consent

(a) Social workers should provide services to clients only in the context of a professional relationship based, when appropriate, on valid informed consent. Social workers should use clear and understandable language to inform clients of the purpose of the services, risks related to the services, limits to services because of the requirements of a third-party payer, relevant costs, reasonable alternatives, clients' right to refuse or withdraw consent, and the time frame covered by the consent. Social workers should provide clients with an opportunity to ask questions.

(b) In instances when clients are not literate or have difficulty understanding the primary language used in the practice setting, social workers should take steps to ensure clients' comprehension. This may include providing clients with a detailed verbal explanation or arranging for a qualified interpreter or translator whenever possible.

(c) In instances when clients lack the capacity to provide informed consent, social workers should protect clients' interests by seeking permission from an appropriate third party, informing clients consistent with the clients' level of understanding. In such instances social workers should seek to ensure that the third party acts in a manner consistent with clients' wishes and interests. Social workers should take reasonable steps to enhance such clients' ability to give informed consent.

(d) In instances when clients are receiving services involuntarily, social workers should provide information about the nature and extent of services and about the extent of clients' right to refuse service.

(e) Social workers who provide services via electronic media (such as computer, telephone, radio, and television) should inform recipients of the limitations and risks associated with such services.

(f) Social workers should obtain clients' informed consent before audiotaping or videotaping clients or permitting observation of services to clients by a third party.

1.04 Competence

(a) Social workers should provide services and represent themselves as competent only within the boundaries of their education, training, license, certification, consultation received, supervised experience, or other relevant professional experience.

(b) Social workers should provide services in substantive areas or use intervention techniques or approaches that are new to them only after engaging in appropriate study, training, consultation, and supervision from people who are competent in those interventions or techniques.

(c) When generally recognized standards do not exist with respect to an emerging area of practice, social workers should exercise careful judgment and take responsible steps (including appropriate education, research, training, consultation, and supervision) to ensure the competence of their work and to protect clients from harm.

1.05 Cultural Competence and Social Diversity

(a) Social workers should understand culture and its function in human behavior and society, recognizing the strengths that exist in all cultures.

(b) Social workers should have a knowledge base of their clients' cultures and be able to demonstrate competence in the provision of services that are sensitive to clients' cultures and to differences among people and cultural groups.

(c) Social workers should obtain education about and seek to understand the nature of social diversity and oppression with respect to race, ethnicity, national origin, color, sex, sexual orientation, age, marital status, political belief, religion, and mental or physical disability.

1.06 Conflicts of Interest

(a) Social workers should be alert to and avoid conflicts of interest that interfere with the exercise of professional discretion and impartial judgment. Social workers should inform clients when a real or potential conflict of interest arises and take reasonable steps to resolve the issue in a manner that makes the clients' interests primary and protects clients' interests to the greatest extent possible. In some cases, protecting clients' interests may require termination of the professional relationship with proper referral of the client.

(b) Social workers should not take unfair advantage of any professional relationship or exploit others to further their personal, religious, political, or business interests.

(c) Social workers should not engage in dual or multiple relationships with clients or former clients in which there is a risk of exploitation or potential harm to the client. In instances when dual or multiple relationships are unavoidable, social workers should take steps to protect clients and are responsible for setting clear, appropriate, and culturally sensitive boundaries. (Dual or multiple relationships occur when social workers relate to clients in more than one relationship, whether professional, social, or business. Dual or multiple relationships can occur simultaneously or consecutively.)

(d) When social workers provide services to two or more people who have a relationship with each other (for example, couples, family members), social workers should clarify with all parties which individuals will be considered clients and the nature of social workers' professional obligations to the various individuals who are receiving services. Social workers who anticipate a conflict of interest among the individuals receiving services or who anticipate having to perform in potentially conflicting roles (for example, when a social worker is asked to testify in a child custody dispute or divorce proceedings involving clients) should clarify their role with the parties involved and take appropriate action to minimize any conflict of interest.

1.07 Privacy and Confidentiality

(a) Social workers should respect clients' right to privacy. Social workers should not solicit private information from clients unless it is essential to providing services or conducting social work evaluation or research. Once private information is shared, standards of confidentiality apply.

(b) Social workers may disclose confidential information when appropriate with valid consent from a client or a person legally authorized to consent on behalf of a client.

(c) Social workers should protect the confidentiality of all information obtained in the course of professional service, except for compelling professional reasons. The general expectation that social workers will keep information confidential does not apply when disclosure is necessary to prevent serious, foreseeable, and imminent harm to a client or other identifiable person. In all instances, social workers should disclose the least amount of confidential information necessary to achieve the desired purpose; only information that is directly relevant to the purpose for which the disclosure is made should be revealed.

(d) Social workers should inform clients, to the extent possible, about the disclosure of confidential information and the potential consequences, when feasible before the disclosure is made. This applies whether social workers disclose confidential information on the basis of a legal requirement or client consent.

(e) Social workers should discuss with clients and other interested parties the nature of confidentiality and limitations of clients' right to confidentiality. Social workers should review with clients circumstances where confidential information may be requested and where disclosure of confidential information may be legally required. This discussion should occur as soon as possible in the social worker-client relationship and as needed throughout the course of the relationship.

(f) When social workers provide counseling services to families, couples, or groups, social workers should seek agreement among the parties involved concerning each individual's right to confidentiality and obligation to preserve the confidentiality of information shared by others. Social workers should inform participants in family, couples, or group counseling that social workers cannot guarantee that all participants will honor such agreements.

(g) Social workers should inform clients involved in family, couples, marital, or group counseling of the social worker's, employer's, and agency's policy concerning the social worker's disclosure of confidential information among the parties involved in the counseling.

(h) Social workers should not disclose confidential information to third-party payers unless clients have authorized such disclosure.

(i) Social workers should not discuss confidential information in any setting unless privacy can be ensured. Social workers should not discuss confidential information in public or semipublic areas such as hallways, waiting rooms, elevators, and restaurants.

(j) Social workers should protect the confidentiality of clients during legal proceedings to the extent permitted by law. When a court of law or other legally authorized body orders social workers to disclose confidential or privileged information without a client's consent and such disclosure could cause harm to the client, social workers should request that the court withdraw the order or limit the order as narrowly as possible or maintain the records under seal, unavailable for public inspection.

(k) Social workers should protect the confidentiality of clients when responding to requests from members of the media.

(l) Social workers should protect the confidentiality of clients' written and electronic records and other sensitive information. Social workers should take reasonable steps to ensure that clients' records are stored in a secure location and that clients' records are not available to others who are not authorized to have access.

(m) Social workers should take precautions to ensure and maintain the confidentiality of information transmitted to other parties through the use of computers, electronic mail, facsimile machines, telephones and telephone answering machines, and other electronic or computer technology. Disclosure of identifying information should be avoided whenever possible.

(n) Social workers should transfer or dispose of clients' records in a manner that protects clients' confidentiality and is consistent with state statutes governing records and social work licensure.

(o) Social workers should take reasonable precautions to protect client confidentiality in the event of the social worker's termination of practice, incapacitation, or death.

(p) Social workers should not disclose identifying information when discussing clients for teaching or training purposes unless the client has consented to disclosure of confidential information.

(q) Social workers should not disclose identifying information when discussing clients with consultants unless the client has consented to disclosure of confidential information or there is a compelling need for such disclosure.

(r) Social workers should protect the confidentiality of deceased clients consistent with the preceding standards.

1.08 Access to Records

(a) Social workers should provide clients with reasonable access to records concerning the clients. Social workers who are concerned that clients' access to their records could cause serious misunderstanding or harm to the client should provide assistance in interpreting the records and consultation with the client regarding the records. Social workers should limit clients' access to their records, or portions of their records, only in exceptional circumstances when there is compelling evidence that such access would cause serious harm to the client. Both clients' requests and the rationale for withholding some or all of the record should be documented in clients' files.

(b) When providing clients with access to their records, social workers should take steps to protect the confidentiality of other individuals identified or discussed in such records.

1.09 Sexual Relationships

(a) Social workers should under no circumstances engage in sexual activities or sexual contact with current clients, whether such contact is consensual or forced.

(b) Social workers should not engage in sexual activities or sexual contact with clients' relatives or other individuals with whom clients maintain a close personal relationship when there is a risk of exploitation or potential harm to the client. Sexual activity or sexual contact with clients' relatives or other individuals with whom clients maintain a personal relationship has the potential to be harmful to the client and may make it difficult for the social worker and client to maintain appropriate professional boundaries. Social workers—not their clients, their clients' relatives, or other individuals with whom the client maintains a personal relationship—assume the full burden for setting clear, appropriate, and culturally sensitive boundaries.

(c) Social workers should not engage in sexual activities or sexual contact with former clients because of the potential for harm to the client. If social workers engage in conduct contrary to this prohibition or claim that an exception to this prohibition is warranted because of extraordinary circumstances, it is social workers—not their clients—who assume the full burden of demonstrating that the former client has not been exploited, coerced, or manipulated, intentionally or unintentionally.

(d) Social workers should not provide clinical services to individuals with whom they have had a prior sexual relationship. Providing clinical services to a former sexual partner has the potential to be harmful to the individual and is likely to make it difficult for the social worker and individual to maintain appropriate professional boundaries.

1.10 Physical Contact

Social workers should not engage in physical contact with clients when there is a possibility of psychological harm to the client as a result of the contact (such as cradling or caressing clients). Social workers who engage in appropriate physical contact with clients are responsible for setting clear, appropriate, and culturally sensitive boundaries that govern such physical contact.

1.11 Sexual Harassment

Social workers should not sexually harass clients. Sexual harassment includes sexual advances, sexual solicitation, requests for sexual favors, and other verbal or physical conduct of a sexual nature.

1.12 Derogatory Language

Social workers should not use derogatory language in their written or verbal communications to or about clients. Social workers should use accurate and respectful language in all communications to and about clients.

1.13 Payment for Services

(a) When setting fees, social workers should ensure that the fees are fair, reasonable, and commensurate with the services performed. Consideration should be given to clients' ability to pay.

(b) Social workers should avoid accepting goods or services from clients as payment for professional services. Bartering arrangements, particularly involving services, create the potential for conflicts of interest, exploitation, and inappropriate boundaries in social workers' relationships with clients. Social workers should explore and may participate in bartering only in very limited circumstances when it can be demonstrated that such arrangements are an accepted practice among professionals in the local community, considered to be essential for the provision of services, negotiated without coercion, and entered into at the client's initiative and with the client's informed consent. Social workers who accept goods or services from clients as payment for professional services assume the full burden of demonstrating that this arrangement will not be detrimental to the client or the professional relationship.

(c) Social workers should not solicit a private fee or other remuneration for providing services to clients who are entitled to such available services through the social workers' employer or agency.

1.14 Clients Who Lack Decision-Making Capacity

When social workers act on behalf of clients who lack the capacity to make informed decisions, social workers should take reasonable steps to safeguard the interests and rights of those clients.

1.15 Interruption of Service

Social workers should make reasonable efforts to ensure continuity of services in the event that services are interrupted by factors such as unavailability, relocation, illness, disability, or death.

1.16 Termination of Services

(a) Social workers should terminate services to clients and professional relationships with them when such services and relationships are no longer required or no longer serve the clients' needs or interests.

(b) Social workers should take reasonable steps to avoid abandoning clients who are still in need of services. Social workers should withdraw services precipitously only under unusual circumstances, giving careful consideration to all factors in the situation and taking care to minimize possible adverse effects. Social workers should assist in making appropriate arrangements for continuation of services when necessary.

(c) Social workers in fee-for-service settings may terminate services to clients who are not paying an overdue balance if the financial contractual arrangements have been made clear to the client, if the client does not pose an imminent danger to self or others, and if the clinical and other consequences of the current nonpayment have been addressed and discussed with the client.

(d) Social workers should not terminate services to pursue a social, financial, or sexual relationship with a client.

(e) Social workers who anticipate the termination or interruption of services to clients should notify clients promptly and seek the transfer, referral, or continuation of services in relation to the clients' needs and preferences.

(f) Social workers who are leaving an employment setting should inform clients of appropriate options for the continuation of services and of the benefits and risks of the options.

2. Social Workers' Ethical Responsibilities to Colleagues
2.01 Respect

(a) Social workers should treat colleagues with respect and should represent accurately and fairly the qualifications, views, and obligations of colleagues.

(b) Social workers should avoid unwarranted negative criticism of colleagues in communications with clients or with other professionals. Unwarranted negative criticism may include demeaning comments that refer to colleagues' level of competence or to individuals' attributes such as race, ethnicity, national origin, color, sex, sexual orientation, age, marital status, political belief, religion, and mental or physical disability.

(c) Social workers should cooperate with social work colleagues and with colleagues of other professions when such cooperation serves the well-being of clients.

2.02 Confidentiality

Social workers should respect confidential information shared by colleagues in the course of their professional relationships and transactions. Social workers should ensure that such colleagues understand social workers' obligation to respect confidentiality and any exceptions related to it.

2.03 Interdisciplinary Collaboration

(a) Social workers who are members of an interdisciplinary team should participate in and contribute to decisions that affect the well-being of clients by drawing on the perspectives, values, and experiences of the social work profession. Professional and ethical obligations of the interdisciplinary team as a whole and of its individual members should be clearly established.

(b) Social workers for whom a team decision raises ethical concerns should attempt to resolve the disagreement through appropriate channels. If the disagreement cannot be resolved, social workers should pursue other avenues to address their concerns consistent with client well-being.

2.04 Disputes Involving Colleagues

(a) Social workers should not take advantage of a dispute between a colleague and an employer to obtain a position or otherwise advance the social workers' own interests.

(b) Social workers should not exploit clients in disputes with colleagues or engage clients in any inappropriate discussion of conflicts between social workers and their colleagues.

2.05 Consultation

(a) Social workers should seek the advice and counsel of colleagues whenever such consultation is in the best interests of clients.

(b) Social workers should keep themselves informed about colleagues' areas of expertise and competencies. Social workers should seek consultation only from colleagues who have demonstrated knowledge, expertise, and competence related to the subject of the consultation.

(c) When consulting with colleagues about clients, social workers should disclose the least amount of information necessary to achieve the purposes of the consultation.

2.06 Referral for Services

(a) Social workers should refer clients to other professionals when the other professionals' specialized knowledge or expertise is needed to serve clients fully or when social workers believe that they are not being effective or making reasonable progress with clients and that additional service is required.

(b) Social workers who refer clients to other professionals should take appropriate steps to facilitate an orderly transfer of responsibility. Social workers who refer clients to other professionals should disclose, with clients' consent, all pertinent information to the new service providers.

(c) Social workers are prohibited from giving or receiving payment for a referral when no professional service is provided by the referring social worker.

2.07 Sexual Relationships

(a) Social workers who function as supervisors or educators should not engage in sexual activities or contact with supervisees, students, trainees, or other colleagues over whom they exercise professional authority.

(b) Social workers should avoid engaging in sexual relationships with colleagues when there is potential for a conflict of interest. Social workers who become involved in, or anticipate becoming involved in, a sexual relationship with a colleague have a duty to transfer professional responsibilities, when necessary, to avoid a conflict of interest.

2.08 Sexual Harassment

Social workers should not sexually harass supervisees, students, trainees, or colleagues. Sexual harassment includes sexual advances, sexual solicitation, requests for sexual favors, and other verbal or physical conduct of a sexual nature.

2.09 Impairment of Colleagues

(a) Social workers who have direct knowledge of a social work colleague's impairment that is due to personal problems, psychosocial distress, substance abuse, or mental health difficulties and that interferes with practice effectiveness should consult with that colleague when feasible and assist the colleague in taking remedial action.

(b) Social workers who believe that a social work colleague's impairment interferes with practice effectiveness and that the colleague has not taken adequate steps to address the impairment should take action through appropriate channels established by employers, agencies, NASW, licensing and regulatory bodies, and other professional organizations.

2.10 Incompetence of Colleagues

(a) Social workers who have direct knowledge of a social work colleague's incompetence should consult with that colleague when feasible and assist the colleague in taking remedial action.

(b) Social workers who believe that a social work colleague is incompetent and has not taken adequate steps to address the incompetence should take action through appropriate channels established by employers, agencies, NASW, licensing and regulatory bodies, and other professional organizations.

2.11 Unethical Conduct of Colleagues

(a) Social workers should take adequate measures to discourage, prevent, expose, and correct the unethical conduct of colleagues.

(b) Social workers should be knowledgeable about established policies and procedures for handling concerns about colleagues' unethical behavior. Social workers should be familiar with national, state, and local procedures for handling ethics complaints. These include policies and procedures created by NASW, licensing and regulatory bodies, employers, agencies, and other professional organizations.

(c) Social workers who believe that a colleague has acted unethically should seek resolution by discussing their concerns with the colleague when feasible and when such discussion is likely to be productive.

(d) When necessary, social workers who believe that a colleague has acted unethically should take action through appropriate formal channels (such as contacting a state licensing board or regulatory body, an NASW committee on inquiry, or other professional ethics committees).

(e) Social workers should defend and assist colleagues who are unjustly charged with unethical conduct.

3. Social Workers' Ethical Responsibilities in Practice Settings
3.01 Supervision and Consultation

(a) Social workers who provide supervision or consultation should have the necessary knowledge and skill to supervise or consult appropriately and should do so only within their areas of knowledge and competence.

(b) Social workers who provide supervision or consultation are responsible for setting clear, appropriate, and culturally sensitive boundaries.

(c) Social workers should not engage in any dual or multiple relationships with supervisees in which there is a risk of exploitation of or potential harm to the supervisee.

(d) Social workers who provide supervision should evaluate supervisees' performance in a manner that is fair and respectful.

3.02 Education and Training

(a) Social workers who function as educators, field instructors for students, or trainers should provide instruction only within their areas of knowledge and competence and should provide instruction based on the most current information and knowledge available in the profession.

(b) Social workers who function as educators or field instructors for students should evaluate students' performance in a manner that is fair and respectful.

(c) Social workers who function as educators or field instructors for students should take reasonable steps to ensure that clients are routinely informed when services are being provided by students.

(d) Social workers who function as educators or field instructors for students should not engage in any dual or multiple relationships with students in which there is a risk of exploitation or potential harm to the student. Social work educators and field instructors are responsible for setting clear, appropriate, and culturally sensitive boundaries.

3.03 Performance Evaluation

Social workers who have responsibility for evaluating the performance of others should fulfill such responsibility in a fair and considerate manner and on the basis of clearly stated criteria.

3.04 Client Records

(a) Social workers should take reasonable steps to ensure that documentation in records is accurate and reflects the services provided.

(b) Social workers should include sufficient and timely documentation in records to facilitate the delivery of services and to ensure continuity of services provided to clients in the future.

(c) Social workers' documentation should protect clients' privacy to the extent that is possible and appropriate and should include only information that is directly relevant to the delivery of services.

(d) Social workers should store records following the termination of services to ensure reasonable future access. Records should be maintained for the number of years required by state statutes or relevant contracts.

3.05 Billing

Social workers should establish and maintain billing practices that accurately reflect the nature and extent of services provided and that identify who provided the service in the practice setting.

3.06 Client Transfer

(a) When an individual who is receiving services from another agency or colleague contacts a social worker for services, the social worker should carefully consider the client's needs before agreeing to provide services. To minimize possible confusion and conflict, social workers should discuss with potential clients the nature of the clients' current relationship with other service providers and the implications, including possible benefits or risks, of entering into a relationship with a new service provider.

(b) If a new client has been served by another agency or colleague, social workers should discuss with the client whether consultation with the previous service provider is in the client's best interest.

3.07 Administration

(a) Social work administrators should advocate within and outside their agencies for adequate resources to meet clients' needs.

(b) Social workers should advocate for resource allocation procedures that are open and fair. When not all clients' needs can be met, an allocation procedure should be developed that is nondiscriminatory and based on appropriate and consistently applied principles.

(c) Social workers who are administrators should take reasonable steps to ensure that adequate agency or organizational resources are available to provide appropriate staff supervision.

(d) Social work administrators should take reasonable steps to ensure that the working environment for which they are responsible is consistent with and encourages compliance with the NASW Code of Ethics. Social work administrators should take reasonable steps to eliminate any conditions in their organizations that violate, interfere with, or discourage compliance with the Code.

3.08 Continuing Education and Staff Development

Social work administrators and supervisors should take reasonable steps to provide or arrange for continuing education and staff development for all staff for whom they are responsible. Continuing education and staff development should address current knowledge and emerging developments related to social work practice and ethics.

3.09 Commitments to Employers

(a) Social workers generally should adhere to commitments made to employers and employing organizations.

(b) Social workers should work to improve employing agencies' policies and procedures and the efficiency and effectiveness of their services.

(c) Social workers should take reasonable steps to ensure that employers are aware of social workers' ethical obligations as set forth in the NASW Code of Ethics and of the implications of those obligations for social work practice.

(d) Social workers should not allow an employing organization's policies, procedures, regulations, or administrative orders to interfere with their ethical practice of social work. Social workers should take reasonable steps to ensure that their employing organizations' practices are consistent with the NASW Code of Ethics.

(e) Social workers should act to prevent and eliminate discrimination in the employing organization's work assignments and in its employment policies and practices.

(f) Social workers should accept employment or arrange student field placements only in organizations that exercise fair personnel practices.

(g) Social workers should be diligent stewards of the resources of their employing organizations, wisely conserving funds where appropriate and never misappropriating funds or using them for unintended purposes.

3.10 Labor-Management Disputes

(a) Social workers may engage in organized action, including the formation of and participation in labor unions, to improve services to clients and working conditions.

(b) The actions of social workers who are involved in labor-management disputes, job actions, or labor strikes should be guided by the profession's values, ethical principles, and ethical standards. Reasonable differences of opinion exist among social workers concerning their primary obligation as professionals during an actual or threatened labor strike or job action. Social workers should carefully examine relevant issues and their possible impact on clients before deciding on a course of action.

4. Social Workers' Ethical Responsibilities as Professionals
4.01 Competence

(a) Social workers should accept responsibility or employment only on the basis of existing competence or the intention to acquire the necessary competence.

(b) Social workers should strive to become and remain proficient in professional practice and the performance of professional functions. Social workers should critically examine and keep current with emerging knowledge relevant to social work. Social workers should routinely review the professional literature and participate in continuing education relevant to social work practice and social work ethics.

(c) Social workers should base practice on recognized knowledge, including empirically based knowledge, relevant to social work and social work ethics.

4.02 Discrimination

Social workers should not practice, condone, facilitate, or collaborate with any form of discrimination on the basis of race, ethnicity, national origin, color, sex, sexual orientation, age, marital status, political belief, religion, or mental or physical disability.

4.03 Private Conduct

Social workers should not permit their private conduct to interfere with their ability to fulfill their professional responsibilities.

4.04 Dishonesty, Fraud, and Deception

Social workers should not participate in, condone, or be associated with dishonesty, fraud, or deception.

4.05 Impairment

(a) Social workers should not allow their own personal problems, psychosocial distress, legal problems, substance abuse, or mental health difficulties to interfere with their professional judgment and performance or to jeopardize the best interests of people for whom they have a professional responsibility.

(b) Social workers whose personal problems, psychosocial distress, legal problems, substance abuse, or mental health difficulties interfere with their professional judgment and performance should immediately seek consultation and take appropriate remedial action by seeking professional help, making adjustments in workload, terminating practice, or taking any other steps necessary to protect clients and others.

4.06 Misrepresentation

(a) Social workers should make clear distinctions between statements made and actions engaged in as a private individual and as a representative of the social work profession, a professional social work organization, or the social worker's employing agency.

(b) Social workers who speak on behalf of professional social work organizations should accurately represent the official and authorized positions of the organizations.

(c) Social workers should ensure that their representations to clients, agencies, and the public of professional qualifications, credentials, education, competence, affiliations, services provided, or results to be achieved are accurate. Social workers should claim only those relevant professional credentials they actually possess and take steps to correct any inaccuracies or misrepresentations of their credentials by others.

4.07 Solicitations

(a) Social workers should not engage in uninvited solicitation of potential clients who, because of their circumstances, are vulnerable to undue influence, manipulation, or coercion.

(b) Social workers should not engage in solicitation of testimonial endorsements (including solicitation of consent to use a client's prior statement as a testimonial endorsement) from current clients or from other people who, because of their particular circumstances, are vulnerable to undue influence.

4.08 Acknowledging Credit

(a) Social workers should take responsibility and credit, including authorship credit, only for work they have actually performed and to which they have contributed.

(b) Social workers should honestly acknowledge the work of and the contributions made by others.

5. Social Workers' Ethical Responsibilities to the Social Work Profession
5.01 Integrity of the Profession

(a) Social workers should work toward the maintenance and promotion of high standards of practice.

(b) Social workers should uphold and advance the values, ethics, knowledge, and mission of the profession. Social workers should protect, enhance, and improve the integrity of the profession through appropriate study and research, active discussion, and responsible criticism of the profession.

(c) Social workers should contribute time and professional expertise to activities that promote respect for the value, integrity, and competence of the social work profession. These activities may include teaching, research, consultation, service, legislative testimony, presentations in the community, and participation in their professional organizations.

(d) Social workers should contribute to the knowledge base of social work and share with colleagues their knowledge related to practice, research, and ethics. Social workers should seek to contribute to the profession's literature and to share their knowledge at professional meetings and conferences.

(e) Social workers should act to prevent the unauthorized and unqualified practice of social work.

5.02 Evaluation and Research

(a) Social workers should monitor and evaluate policies, the implementation of programs, and practice interventions.

(b) Social workers should promote and facilitate evaluation and research to contribute to the development of knowledge.

(c) Social workers should critically examine and keep current with emerging knowledge relevant to social work and fully use evaluation and research evidence in their professional practice.

(d) Social workers engaged in evaluation or research should carefully consider possible consequences and should follow guidelines developed for the protection of evaluation and research participants. Appropriate institutional review boards should be consulted.

(e) Social workers engaged in evaluation or research should obtain voluntary and written informed consent from participants, when appropriate, without any implied or actual deprivation or penalty for refusal to participate; without undue inducement to participate; and with due regard for participants' well-being, privacy, and dignity. Informed consent should include information about the nature, extent, and duration of the participation requested and disclosure of the risks and benefits of participation in the research.

(f) When evaluation or research participants are incapable of giving informed consent, social workers should provide an appropriate explanation to the participants, obtain the participants' assent to the extent they are able, and obtain written consent from an appropriate proxy.

(g) Social workers should never design or conduct evaluation or research that does not use consent procedures, such as certain forms of naturalistic observation and archival research, unless rigorous and responsible review of the research has found it to be justified because of its prospective scientific, educational, or applied value and unless equally effective alternative procedures that do not involve waiver of consent are not feasible.

(h) Social workers should inform participants of their right to withdraw from evaluation and research at any time without penalty.

(i) Social workers should take appropriate steps to ensure that participants in evaluation and research have access to appropriate supportive services.

(j) Social workers engaged in evaluation or research should protect participants from unwarranted physical or mental distress, harm, danger, or deprivation.

(k) Social workers engaged in the evaluation of services should discuss collected information only for professional purposes and only with people professionally concerned with this information.

(l) Social workers engaged in evaluation or research should ensure the anonymity or confidentiality of participants and of the data obtained from them. Social workers should inform participants of any limits of confidentiality, the measures that will be taken to ensure confidentiality, and when any records containing research data will be destroyed.

(m) Social workers who report evaluation and research results should protect participants' confidentiality by omitting identifying information unless proper consent has been obtained authorizing disclosure.

(n) Social workers should report evaluation and research findings accurately. They should not fabricate or falsify results and should take steps to correct any errors later found in published data using standard publication methods.

(o) Social workers engaged in evaluation or research should be alert to and avoid conflicts of interest and dual relationships with participants, should inform participants when a real or potential conflict of interest arises, and should take steps to resolve the issue in a manner that makes participants' interests primary.

(p) Social workers should educate themselves, their students, and their colleagues about responsible research practices.

6. Social Workers' Ethical Responsibilities to the Broader Society
6.01 Social Welfare

Social workers should promote the general welfare of society, from local to global levels, and the development of people, their communities, and their environments. Social workers should advocate for living conditions conducive to the fulfillment of basic human needs and should promote social, economic, political, and cultural values and institutions that are compatible with the realization of social justice.

6.02 Public Participation

Social workers should facilitate informed participation by the public in shaping social policies and institutions.

6.03 Public Emergencies

Social workers should provide appropriate professional services in public emergencies to the greatest extent possible.

6.04 Social and Political Action

(a) Social workers should engage in social and political action that seeks to ensure that all people have equal access to the resources, employment, services, and opportunities they require to meet their basic human needs and to develop fully. Social workers should be aware of the impact of the political arena on practice and should advocate for changes in policy and legislation to improve social conditions in order to meet basic human needs and promote social justice.

(b) Social workers should act to expand choice and opportunity for all people, with special regard for vulnerable, disadvantaged, oppressed, and exploited people and groups.

(c) Social workers should promote conditions that encourage respect for cultural and social diversity within the United States and globally. Social workers should promote policies and practices that demonstrate respect for difference, support the expansion of cultural knowledge and resources, advocate for programs and institutions that demonstrate cultural competence, and promote policies that safeguard the rights of and confirm equity and social justice for all people.

(d) Social workers should act to prevent and eliminate domination of, exploitation of, and discrimination against any person, group, or class on the basis of race, ethnicity, national origin, color, sex, sexual orientation, age, marital status, political belief, religion, or mental or physical disability.

Notes

Preface

1. American Psychiatric Association, *Diagnostic and Statistical Manual of Mental Disorders*, 4th ed. (Washington, D.C.: American Psychiatric Association, 1994).

2. Spiegel, Alix, "The Dictionary of Disorder," *The New Yorker*, January 3, 2005, p. 61.

3. The authors made some projections on potential sales of DSM-IV-TR based on membership obtained from the web sites of the four national professional organizations: the American Psychiatric Association (35,000); the American Psychological Association, (150,000); the National Association of Social Workers (153,000); and the American Association of Marriage, Family Therapists (23,000). Multiplying the number of members by the cost of the primary manual (361,000 × 64.00) yields a figure of $23,164,000.00 for the sale of just one out of the 41 titles available from the publisher. This does not include sales to students who are attending Universities to acquire degrees in mental health services, or studying for licensure. Nor does this figure include persons who operate in human service industries related to mental health, drug prevention, women's shelters, vocational rehabilitation, private medical and psychiatric facilities, and many others that we can't even begin to imagine.

4. Conversation with representative of American Psychiatric Association.

Chapter 2

1. Goffman, Erving, *Asylums* (New York: Anchor Books, 1961), p. 378 ff.

Chapter 3

1. National Association of Social Workers (1999). *Code of Ethics.* Washington, D.C.: NASW.

2. Codes of Ethics may be accessed on-line at the following URLs:

(a) American Association of Marriage, Family Therapists, www.aamft.org/re sources/lrmplan/ethics/ethicscode2001.asp

(b) American Psychiatric Association, www.apa.org/

(c) American Psychological Association, www.apa.org/ethics/

(d) National Association of Social Workers, www.socialworkers.org/pubs/code/code.asp

Chapter 4

1. American Psychiatric Association, *op. cit.*, p. 424.

Chapter 5

1. World Health Organization, *International Classification of Functioning, Disability and Health* (Geneva, Switzerland: World Health Organization, 2001).

Chapter 6

1. The Health Insurance Portability and Accountability Act of 1996. PL 104–191 (HIPAA), can be accessed at: www.cms.hhs.gov/hipaa/.
2. Kalish, M. (2004, July) National Association of Social Workers, California News, p. 10.
3. USA Patriot Act of 2001, can be accessed at: www.epic.org/privacy/terrorism/hr3162.html.
4. NASW *Current Controversies in Social Work Ethics: Case Examples*, NASW Press, 1998, p. 51.
5. Simply put, that the client recognizes the basis of his/her difficulty. See, for example Basch, Michael Franz, *Doing Psychotherapy* (New York: Basic Books, 1980), p. 171.

Chapter 7

1. The Americans with Disabilities Act of 1990, PL 101–336 (ADA) can be accessed at: www.usdoj.gov/crt/ada/adahom1.htm.

Myth II. Introduction

1. American Psychiatric Association, *op. cit.*, pp. 680–686.

Chapter 8

1. American Psychiatric Association: *Diagnostic and Statistical Manual of Mental Disorders*, 4th ed. (Washington, D.C.: American Psychiatric Association, 1994).
2. *Ibid.*
3. *Ibid.*, p. xxiii; "It is important that DSM-IV not be applied mechanically by untrained individuals. The specific diagnostic criteria included in DSM-IV are meant to serve as guidelines to be informed by clinical judgment and are not to be used in a cookbook fashion."
4. Goffman, Erving, *Stigma* (Englewood Cliffs, N.J.: Prentice-Hall, 1963), p. 4.
5. Szasz, Thomas, *The Myth of Mental Illness*, rev. ed. (New York: Harper and Row, 1974).
6. American Psychiatric Association, *op. cit.*, p. 25.
7. *Ibid.*, p. 680 ff for V codes.

Chapter 10

1. American Psychiatric Association, *op.cit.*, pp. 46–53. (LD)
2. *Ibid.*, pp. 78–85. (AD/HD)
3. *Ibid.*, pp. 46–53. (LDs for clinical psychologists)
4. Kubiszyn, Tom, and Gary Borich, *Educational Testing and Measurement: classroom Application and Practice*, 3rd ed. (HarperCollins, 1990), p. 389.
5. Lewis, Rena B., and Donald H. Doorlag, *Teaching Special Students in the Mainstream*, 3rd ed. (New York: Merrill, 1991), pp. 233–4.
6. Quinn, Patricia O., ed., *ADD and the College Student* (New York: Magination Press, 1994), p. 99.

7. *Ibid.*, p. 102.

8. Vogel, Susan A., *College Students with Learning Disabilities* (Northern Illinois University, 1993), p. 3 ff.

9. Kavale, K., and Forness, S., "What Definitions of Learning Disability Say and Don't Say," *Journal of Learning Disabilities,* 33 (May/June, 2000), 239–256.

10. Blalock, G., and Patton, J., "Transition and Students with Learning Disabilities: Creating Sound Futures," *Journal of Learning Disabilities* (January, 1996), 1–37.

11. Brinkerhoff, L., "Making the Transition to Higher Education: Opportunities for Student Empowerment," *Journal of Learning Disabilities* (March, 1996), 118–137.

12. Dowdy, C., "Vocational Rehabilitation and Special Education: Partners in Transition for Individuals with Learning Disabilities," *Journal of Learning Disabilities* (March, 1996), 113–136.

Chapter 14

1. Leech, Peter, and Zeva Singer, *Acknowledgment: Opening to the Grief of Unacceptable Loss* (Laytonville, Calif.: Wintercreek Publications, 1988), p. 13.

Chapter 15

1. Leech, Peter, and Zeva Singer, *Acknowledgment: Opening to the Grief of Unacceptable Loss* (Laytonville, Calif.: Wintercreek Publications, 1988).

Chapter 16

1. Mattaini, Mark A., Christine T. Lowery and Carol H. Meyer, eds., *The Foundations of Social Work Practice: A Graduate Text* (Washington, D.C.: National Association of Social Workers, 1998), p. 3.

2. World Health Organization, *International Classification of Functioning, Disability and Health* (Geneva, Switzerland: World Health Organization, 2001).

Myth III. Introduction

1. Ralph Dolgoff, Donald Feldstein and Louise Skolnick, *Understanding Social Welfare,* 4th ed. (White Plains, N.Y.: Longman, 1997), p. 59 ff.

Myth IV. Introduction

1. Spiegel, Alix, "The Dictionary of Disorder," *The New Yorker,* January 3, 2005, p. 58.

2. *Ibid.*, p. 63.

3. Copyright 1999, National Association of Social Workers, Inc., NASW Code of Ethics.

Chapter 23

1. Ralph Dolgoff, Donald Feldstein and Louise Skolnick, *Understanding Social Welfare,* 4th ed. (White Plains, N.Y.: Longman, 1997), pp. 51–53.

2. *Ibid.*, pp. 66–67.

3. Goffman, Erving, *Asylums,* presents convincing perspectives that support moving away from the notion that all behavior must be viewed as residual of a mental disorder.

Chapter 24

1. Goffman, Erving, *Asylums.*

2. Szasz, Thomas, *The Myth of Mental Illness*, rev. ed. (New York: Harper and Row, 1974), p. 262.

3. Excerpted from interview with Pernille Gildsig, Psychologist, Denmark.

4. Excerpted from conversation with resident of Calgary, Alberta, Canada.

5. Excerpted from conversation with native of New Zealand.

Chapter 25

1. Dolgoff, et al., *op. cit.*, pp. 266–267.

2. *Ibid.*, p. 267.

Bibliography

American Psychiatric Association. *Diagnostic and Statistical Manual of Mental Disorders*, 4th ed. Washington, D.C.: American Psychiatric Association, 1994.

Americans with Disabilities Act of 1990. PL 101–336 (ADA) can be accessed at: www.usdoj.gov/crt/ada/adahom1.htm

Basch, Michael Franz. *Doing Psychotherapy*. New York: Basic Books, 1980.

Blalock, G., and J. Patton. "Transition and Students with Learning Disabilities: Creating Sound Futures." *Journal of Learning*, January 1996.

Brinkerhoff, L. "Making the Transition to Higher Education: Opportunities for Student Empowerment." *Journal of Learning Disabilities, 29* (March 1996), 118–137.

Codes of Ethics may be accessed on-line at the following URLs: a. The American Association of Marriage, Family Therapists: www.aamft.org/resources/lrmplan/ethics/ethicscode2001.asp; b. The American Psychiatric Association: www.psych.org/psych_pract/ethics/ethics.cfm; b. The American Psychological Association: www.apa.org/ethics/; c. National Association of Social Workers: www.socialworkers.org/pubs/code/code.asp

Dolgoff, Ralph, Donald Feldstein, and Louise Skolnick. *Understanding Social Welfare*, 4th ed. White Plains, N.Y.: Longman, 1997.

Dowdy, C. "Vocational Rehabilitation and Special Education: Partners in Transition for Individuals with Learning Disabilities." *Journal of Learning Disabilities, 29* (March 1996), 113–136.

Goffman, Erving, *Asylums.* New York: Anchor Books, 1961.

_____. *Stigma.* Englewood Cliffs, N.J.: Prentice-Hall, 1963.

Health Insurance Portability and Accountability Act of 1996. PL 104–191 (HIPAA), can be accessed at: www.cms.hhs.gov/hipaa/.

Kalish, M. "National Association of Social Workers," *California News.* July 2004.

Kavale, K. & Forness, S. "What Definitions of Learning Disability Say and Don't Say." *Journal of Learning Disabilities, 33* (May/June 2000), 239–256.

Kubiszyn, Tom, and Gary Borich. *Educational Testing and Measurement: Classroom Application and Practice*, 3rd ed. USA: Harper Collins, 1990.

Kutchins, Herb, and Stuart Kirk. *Making Us Crazy, DSM: The Psychiatric Bible and the Creation of Mental Disorders.* New York: Free Press, 1997.

Leech, Peter, and Zeva Singer. *Acknowledgment: Opening to the Grief of Unacceptable Loss.* Laytonville, Calif.: Wintercreek Publications, 1988.

Lewis, Rena B., and Donald H. Doorlag. *Teaching Special Students in the Mainstream,* 3rd ed. New York: Merrill, 1991.

Mattaini, Mark A., Christine T. Lowery, and Carol H. Meyer, eds. *The Foundations of Social Work Practice: A Graduate Text.* Washington, D.C.: National Association of Social Workers, 1998.

National Association of Social Workers. *Code of Ethics.* Washington, D.C.: NASW, 1996.

_____. *Current Controversies in Social Work Ethics: Case Examples.* Washington, D.C.: NASW Press, 1998.

Quinn, Patricia O., ed. *ADD and the College Student.* New York: Magination Press, 1994.

Spiegel, Alix. "The Dictionary of Disorder," *The New Yorker,* January 3, 2005.

Szasz, Thomas S. *The Myth of Mental Illness,* rev. ed. New York: Harper and Row, 1974.

USA Patriot Act of 2001, can be accessed at: www.epic.org/privacy/terrorism/hr3162.html.

Vogel, Susan A. *College Students with Learning Disabilities.* Northern Illinois University, 1993.

World Health Organization. *International Classification of Functioning, Disability and Health.* Geneva, Switzerland: World Health Organization, 2001.

Index